Maurice Rosenblatt

and | *the fall of*
Joseph McCarthy

Maurice Rosenblatt

and *the fall of*
Joseph McCarthy

Shelby Scates

To Roj.
Best Regards
—and good reading

University of Washington Press
SEATTLE AND LONDON

in association with

History Ink
SEATTLE

History Ink
www.historylink.org
1425 4th Avenue Ste 710
Seattle, WA 98101

University of Washington Press
P.O. Box 50096, Seattle, WA 98145
www.washington.edu/uwpress

Library of Congress Cataloging-in-Publication Data

Scates, Shelby
Maurice Rosenblatt and the fall of Joseph McCarthy/
Shelby Scates. p. cm
Includes bioliographical references and index.
ISBN 0-295-98594-1 (pbk.: alk. paper)
1. McCarthy, Joseph, 1908 – 1957—Adversaries.
2. Rosenblatt, Maurice. 3. Army–McCarthy
Controversy, 1954. 4. United States—Politics and
government—1945–1953. 5. United States—Politics
and government—1953–1961. I. Title.
E748.M143S28 2005
973.921'092—dc22   2005030042

"Someone must have been telling lies about Joseph K.,
for without having done anything wrong he was arrested one
fine morning." And a few days later, the Police Inspector:
"I can't even confirm you are charged with an offense,
or rather, I don't know if you are. You are under arrest,
more than that I do not know."

—Franz Kafka, *The Trial,* 1937

Contents

Prologue

MY LIFE AS A MERCHANT SEAMAN in the early 1950s came with adventure, discovery, and intense political discussion. It was a pivotal time in United States history, the peak of the demagogic power of Joe McCarthy and the end of Communist influence on West Coast waterfronts—coincidence, not consequence.

There was much to talk about in the engine rooms of vessels where I worked, and time to do it. A likely conversational starting point was the 1934 West Coast maritime strike, which led to enormous improvements in the conditions under which we labored—wages, quarters, meals—for which we were grateful. All veteran hands acknowledged that Communists had led the strike yet failed to gain from its triumph union leadership, much less a first blow in an American revolution. Now, back East, Senator Joe McCarthy was portraying himself, and was being portrayed, as the only force averting Communist domination of our government—and woe to those who dared question him.

Most of what I have just written is long forgotten, if it was ever much known. History moves on. So did I, as a soldier and journalist. Decades later, researching a biography of Senator Warren Magnuson, I went to lunch with Maurice Rosenblatt in his brownstone mansion on New Jersey Avenue in Washington, D.C., a few blocks from the Capitol.

A mutual friend, Joe Miller, a Seattle newsman turned Washington labor lobbyist, brought us together, and as my fellow sailors and I had done in the ship's fireroom, we began talking politics. We didn't quit until suppertime. There was a theme: the extreme stresses placed on American democracy by both the left and the right from 1930 to the climax of McCarthyism in 1955, when real and imagined threats fractured civility, making more victims of innocents than of the guilty. It was a time better described by Franz Kafka than by the *New York Times*. How did democracy and civility survive?

Rosenblatt, a successful lobbyist for nonscheduled airlines, I learned that day, had been a participant in the political action of that turbulent period, a street organizer against New York City's right-wing toughs, a lobbyist for U.S. recognition of the State of Israel, and the man who orchestrated the undoing of Joe McCarthy. He was one who helped preserve democracy and civility.

My much admired union compatriot Bob Casey organized and led the last serious effort of the left—in this case anti-Communist Trotskyites—to take control of a West Coast waterfront local. A rigid ideologue, he failed, which perhaps added to his contempt for "liberals—good only for writing books." But Casey never met Maurice, or anyone quite like him.

Few Americans remain like Rosenblatt who experienced, even remotely, those mid-century political travails. Like his sometime colleague, the writer Ben Hecht, he was a "child of the twentieth century." Even rarer, he was an American participant and activist in a roiling stretch of political history.

From this introduction, I sized Rosenblatt up as a bare-knuckled Ralph Nader, a political organizer comfortable on the streets or in the boardrooms, a liberal, not a zealot, with a personality of velvet and steel. He had a ready sense of humor, a feature usually lacking in ship's forecastles. I was set on meeting him again and soon did so for more political history. What follows came from those talks.

What I learned was this: while history may flow of its own gravity, apparently inexorably, it may be shaped in its course by individuals of exceptionally strong will and high intelligence, an uncommon combination. Maurice Rosenblatt fit the bill: a determined democrat who faced men of great zeal and ruthlessness—from the streets of New York to the corridors of Congress, from Father Charles Coughlin with his anti-Semitic "Christian Front" to Joe McCarthy—men who would have put aside, if not scorned, the due processes given Americans by their Constitution, and stood them down.

Some suggest that McCarthy was his own worst enemy. If so, Rosenblatt was his close rival.

And thus, this narrative.

1 | The Carroll Arms and the National Committee for an Effective Congress

IT'S GONE NOW, save in the vivid memories of a few old-timers who lived, worked, and played around Capitol Hill in twentieth-century Washington, D.C. The Carroll Arms Hotel and its basement bar, kitty-corner from the old Senate Office Building, was destroyed in 1974, displaced by a parking lot and, post–September 11, 2001, by the ugly juxtaposition of concrete barriers and armed police. Fear of terrorism had replaced the terror of McCarthyism, a legacy of a frequent guest, Senator Joseph McCarthy, R-Wisconsin.

Mark Russell, the political satirist, played the barroom piano at the Carroll Arms in the 1950s and cracked inside jokes as senators, congressmen, and their aides and sweethearts (some-times one and the same) came to lunch at noon and to drink in the late afternoon. He was very funny. Once asked if he had any writers for his material, Russell said, "Yes, 535 writers—100 in the Senate, 435 in the House of Representatives." Scores of these he entertained.[1]

Sometimes it seemed as if the nation's Capitol had shifted across the street to the Carroll Arms bar. Woody Price, an aide to transportation secretary Brock Adams, recalled one early afternoon, standing room only, aides and congressmen pressed against each other for a two-hour lunch. An Appropriations Committee staffer, Stewart McClure, raised his voice above the tumult to remark, "If a bomb obliterated this place right now, the work of the United States Senate would be delayed by—thirty seconds!" Another round followed.[2]

This was a political no-man's-land, a listening post at First and C Streets Northeast that might be likened to neutral Lisbon during World War II. Senator Barry Goldwater, looking ahead to

1964 and a run for the White House, installed a lawyer pal from Phoenix, Denison Kitchel, in an office in the six-story Carroll Arms under the sham label "Goldwater for Senate." Goldwater's instructions: "Keep your powder dry and listen to everybody. We'll take to the end of 1963 to evaluate the [presidential] political situation."[3] Goldwater would run and lose the 1964 election to Lyndon Johnson.

By 1972, an expanding Congress needed extra room and resorted to the hotel. The first home of the Congressional Budget Office, creature of a budget reform act engineered by Senator Ed Muskie and then Representative Brock Adams, was a leaky room with a three-legged desk in the hotel basement, adjacent to the bar. As late as 1961 a single room could be had at the Carroll Arms for $10 a night. Perhaps it, too, leaked.

Bobby Baker, the Senate majority secretary and prince of Capitol wheeler-dealer-fixers, formed and ran the "Quorum Club," members only, mostly lobbyists selected by Bobby himself. This was above the bar on the hotel's second floor. You could learn about the current barroom lineup from the woman at the lobby newsstand. Otherwise, she wasn't very well informed: she thought Joe McCarthy was a liberal.[4]

Before wrecking balls took it down in 1974, reporters got stories in the Carroll Arms bar, only a few of them fit to print, the line between the public and private affairs of elected officials not yet having been shattered in American journalism. Roy Cohn and G. David Schine, aides-extraordinaire to Senator McCarthy, chairman of the Senate Permanent Subcommittee on Investigations, lived together in a top-floor suite. According to Rosenblatt, they regularly came downstairs in the afternoon to drink with their boss and with Don Surine, a defrocked FBI agent turned subcommittee investigator.

The Carroll Arms began as a "railroad hotel" to accommodate travelers detraining from Union Station, a long walk or a short cab ride up the avenue. It would become backstage to the theater of Joe McCarthy, the high political drama soon to be playing across the street on the Senate floor and in the Senate caucus room, spreading from there onto the front pages of newspapers and through coast-to-coast television into the living rooms of America—a drama the likes of which many had never seen before and would never see again.

When Mark Russell played the piano, not everyone applauded. Some of his political satire must have smacked too close to home. "It really did upset some of them," he said years later. "But in those days there was no satire on television, no irreverence. The barometer was good old Bob Hope. It was the McCarthy era. He had lived in the hotel."

One flight below McCarthy's aides, Cohn and Schine, in a remarkable juxtaposition of friend and foe, if not beauty and beast, Maurice Rosenblatt, late of Vienna, Madison, New York, and New Guinea, shared a suite with the lovely and intelligent Laura Barone, formerly of Monette, Missouri, lately of the John Powers model agency in Manhattan. Laura was Rosenblatt's love and invaluable aide in his increasingly successful lobbying jobs on Capitol Hill. She was a sure-fire means of breaching congressional offices, even those most resistant. Bill Knowland, the new GOP Senate majority leader? No problem. "Laura would get chased around the desk two or three times," said Maurice, "but she would get the message to Knowland."

Having found a postwar home and occupation in Washington, smart, handsome Maurice Rosenblatt needed access. He had closed the doors to his previous organization, the American League for Free Palestine—a driving force behind President Harry Truman's fateful decision to recognize the new State of Israel—and was off and running with a lobbying business. His major clients: nonscheduled airlines. They were a new breed of wildcat operations featuring World War II aviators and surplus Air Force transports. Think of all those unused Douglas C-47s and unemployed hotshot pilots.

Rosenblatt, his former associates suggest, was earning a lot of money, but something was missing. For an athlete, long-distance runner, mountain climber, or war lover, the diagnosis would have been clinically easy: an absence of the adrenaline that accompanies high excitement. Perhaps it was the same for Maurice. After watching Nazi mobs on the streets of Vienna, combating anti-Semitic thugs on the streets of New York, and, with Ben Hecht and others concerned about Jewish survivors of the Holocaust, pushing for the creation of Israel, Rosenblatt needed a fix. He jumped back into high-stakes political action.

As Maurice would come to explain, he worried about the 1946 crop of congressmen, too many of them eager to turn the country away from "foreign entanglements." They began to crystallize around Knowland's predecessor as majority leader, Senator Robert Taft of Ohio. It appeared to Rosenblatt like a rebirth of the America First Committee, which had opposed American intervention in World War II—isolationism all over again. "Did we win the war only to lose the peace?" he asked companions. What loomed was another cause in need of a political organizer's attention.

The upshot was that with Harry Selden, Stewart McClure, and George Agree, old political friends and allies in his earlier political organizations, Rosenblatt formed the National Committee for an Effective Congress (NCEC). The four quickly recruited a nucleus of political and financial support. Eleanor Roosevelt, the president's widow, was a prime recruit.[5] Others included Elliott and Faye Emerson Roosevelt; Harley Kilgore, a West Virginia senator close to President Truman; Oscar Chapman, former secretary of the interior; and Oscar Hammerstein II, the Broadway librettist.

The new committee rustled up $1,000 in seed money from Bernard Baruch, the New York financier and presidential confidante, and carefully screened potential members, nervous over the possibility of Communist infiltration. This was 1948, when such a possibility was perceived to be real. Rosenblatt's aversion to Communist Party members was visceral. He had known them in Manhattan in the 1930s and believed they could not be trusted.[6]

Mary Lasker, wife of the Madison Avenue advertising tycoon Albert Lasker, would help, too—in more ways than one. She gave money, but as a "Knickerbocker" New Yorker she also lent the cause high-society connections and credibility. The "Irish girl from Watertown, Wisconsin," as Rosenblatt called her, had married well.

Baruch was an angel for such liberal causes, a man with enormous wealth and an ego to match. "He wanted you to know," said Rosenblatt, a recipient of the angel's largess, "that he invented everything in politics. FDR did not consider Baruch loyal—he played too many games." But with Baruch's help, the NCEC became the liberal response to the challenge from the "radical right," a term Rosenblatt's associate Russ Hemenway claims Maurice coined.

"We were sure [New York Governor Tom] Dewey would beat Truman in the 1948 election and that would bring in on his coattails an isolationist Senate that would keep us out of the United Nations the way [Massachusetts Senator Henry Cabot] Lodge kept us out of the League of Nations in 1920," said Harry Selden about the NCEC. "So we looked over a list of thirty-three Senate races and chose six we thought could be held by good men who would thwart any isolationist attempt. We raised some money, but it was technical assistance that was important."

For the first organizational meeting, held at the Madison Hotel in Washington, Mrs. Roosevelt sent her son James, a conspicuously unsung hero of World War II, executive officer of a Marine commando battalion commanded by Colonel Evans Carlson. "Carlson's Raiders" fought with knives, shotguns, and piano wire, securing beachheads on Japanese-held islands in the South Pacific. Beloved by their troops, Roosevelt and Carlson went different ways after the war,[9] Roosevelt eventually to Congress, and Carlson to an undeserved oblivion. Though a great soldier, he was politically suspect for his appreciation of the tactics of Mao Tse-tung and Chu Teh's Eighth Route Army, spearhead of China's Communist revolution. He had adapted those tactics—move fast, travel light—to the raider battalion.

James Roosevelt became first chairman of the NCEC, a liberal, nonpartisan, internationalist organization with a board resembling a New Deal alumni gathering, most prominent being the Roosevelts, Chapman, and Harold Ickes. George Agree ran the New York office. Rosenblatt was executive director in Washington, his office in the Carroll Arms. Mrs. Roosevelt signed the first fundraising letters, which yielded wherewithal for the campaigns.

Rosenblatt with his finely honed political talents was at the brink of his most significant achievements: playing a critical role in the election of six liberal senators and orchestrating the undoing of Senator Joe McCarthy. Like his actions in 1938 in New York City's Bronx, where he had pitted a dozen Christian divinity students against a howling mob of "Coughlinites"—anti-Semitic followers of Father Charles Coughlin—these were further exercises in political jujitsu, the art of leveraging minimum strength against maximum force. By 1948, Maurice was a political jujitsu artist.

The committee had to work fast. Elections were coming, and President Truman loomed as a sure loser. But the new organization clicked. It looked east and west for contributions and down the nation's middle for Senate candidates. It aimed to get the most for its money, and campaigns cost less in smaller states. It also wanted candidates concerned with the nation's world policy. By design, the NCEC was a counterforce to the new Republican isolationists.

When it was done, Truman had been reelected. The NCEC had been a critical factor in the election of hard-core liberal, internationalist senators who would endure for nearly two decades. Rosenblatt could take a bow. "He had a jeweler's eye for political talent," said Joe Miller.

"The National Committee for an Effective Congress' assistance to liberal candidates in key states was a decisive factor in [our] election victories. . . . it was practical, down-to-earth activity. Impressive." So wrote the new Senate members, Hubert Humphrey, Estes Kefauver, Matthew Neeley, Guy Gillette, Jim Murray, and Paul Douglas, in their thank-you letter to the NCEC board.[10]

These were tough campaigns. Humphrey, the future vice president and 1968 Democratic presidential nominee, defeated an extremely well-financed incumbent, Joe Ball. Kefauver, a Southern anomaly—liberal, intellectual—beat Boss Ed Crump's Tennessee machine. That was the Portland Beavers beating the New York Yankees. Crump ran his state the way Anaconda ran Montana, but the mining giant also lost. It couldn't defeat the aging Jim Murray, up for reelection in that state.

"We ran the committee out of my back pocket," Rosenblatt would recall. "The six candidates were all strong public leaders, a forward-looking bloc. The committee kept a very low profile. Otherwise it might have been a liability in the South and West. Elliott Roosevelt rang doorbells for money. He had to, given our shortage. The Democratic National Committee put everything into Truman's race, nothing for Congress."

Members of the committee met with the potential candidates in the Mayflower Hotel. Rosenblatt described them as a congenial lot, wary of concentrated wealth and economic power, pro–civil rights, and "respectful of the opinions of others." They were pragmatic liberals, not dogmatic. They were the committee's core force to prevent capture of the Senate by the GOP's radical right wing.

Oddly, in light of what would become a viciously divisive issue in the 1950s, events in China, where the U.S.–backed and generously funded Nationalist government was getting whipped in a civil war by Chinese Communists, failed to surface in these campaigns. "Not on the agenda," said Rosenblatt, their master Democratic architect. "Unlike the matter of Israel, which people took personally and whose arguments could break up dinner parties, China wasn't controversial. It wasn't much known aside from select sophisticates and maybe readers of Max Ascoli's *Reporter* magazine."

On election eve, 1948, Rosenblatt gathered with others at Manhattan's Chatham Hotel on Forty-ninth Street near Grand Central Station to await returns. He took a call from Charles Rose, an Associated Press political reporter. Rose asked which of the six NCEC candidates would win. Rosenblatt answered, "All six." Rose asked if he'd bet his life on that prediction. Rosenblatt paused to review each contest and again answered, "All six." They did.

"That," Maurice wrote in a letter to Selden forty-five years later, "was a night to remember!"[11]

Rosenblatt worked behind the scenes: "If I had been overly visible it would have been detrimental." From offstage he placed NCEC money where it counted. A $1,000 contribution in Tennessee, Iowa, or Montana had more pop than a $5,000 contribution in New York or California. Political jujitsu—maximum force from minimum energy—in this case, money. In Minnesota, a wad—$12,000—was spent on ads reprinting a rundown of Ball's fat-cat contributors.

Maurice took no pay for his work. Compensation would come later, only slightly indirectly, in the form of the help he would get for his lobbying clients from the senators he helped elect. He took some critical heat for this and, pressed, would answer with a question: If a lobbyist can't call on political friends, to whom does he turn?

Boss Crump was unforgiving. So were Tennessee segregationists—a vast majority, especially in West Tennessee, where it was heard said in 1959, when Kefauver had to campaign again, "If that nigger-lover Kefauver comes to town he's liable to get shot." Joe Miller, a sometime business associate of Maurice's and a Democratic campaign operative, heard the grim news and early in 1960 went to Nashville to Kefauver's campaign headquarters at the Andrew Jackson Hotel near the state Capitol. "Aw, don't worry none, Joe," said a local staffer, pouring his nervous visitor a glass of bourbon. "When Ole Estes comes home from the Congress, he'll put a whiskey bottle in one hand, a girl on the other, go up to them hills and get every county."[12] He almost did. But he also carried the overtly hostile west Tennessee counties, a triumph of the senator's strength in county courthouses and his native charm over racist attitudes. An unusual admirer, Teddy White of Boston, Jack Kennedy's campaign Boswell, once said that Estes Kefauver was the best president we never had.[13]

Despite its low profile, word spread about the NCEC, at least among the Washington cognoscenti—Congress and the press, particularly the right-wing press, which was Republican, world wary, and Commie conscious. The 1948 election of Harry Truman and the "NCEC Senate Six" halted the right-wing Republican rush into Festung Amerika isolationism, but not the postwar forces behind it.

Joseph McCarthy, not the NCEC, would be preeminent in the 1950 elections, comeback time for the Republican Party after its 1948 thrashing. From being a Senate nobody, generally shunned by other members, McCarthy, although little respected, became very much feared. With fear installed, who needs respect? He would come to claim that he had Rosenblatt and his NCEC group "booted out of the Carroll Arms." Nonsense, said Rosenblatt, who would remain there until the wrecking ball struck the building. "Another wild, unsubstantiated McCarthy charge."

The NCEC continues to the present, with Rosenblatt serving as chairman emeritus until his death in 2005, but its influence on election results would never be so significant as in its initial effort in 1948. Where it would exert its greatest force was in the conflict with Joe McCarthy.

2 | Tailgunner Joe, Chanker Jack, and "Moose Dung"

AT MID-TWENTIETH CENTURY, there wasn't much to remark in the life of Joe McCarthy, except that he held a U.S. Senate seat and wanted badly to keep it. To grasp his means for doing so—and then doing more—one must turn from Wisconsin to China and go back in time a few years.

American policy in China in the 1930s and 1940s—"the great American illusion," as Winston Churchill called it[1]—was essential raw material for McCarthy and McCarthyism, the stuff on which, more than anything, he debuted his campaign against alleged Communist subversion in a Lincoln Day speech on February 9, 1950, in Wheeling, West Virginia.

"I have in my hand a list of two hundred and five," said Joe, "a list of names that were made known to the secretary of state as being members of the Communist Party and who, nevertheless are still working and shaping policy in the State Department."[2] And never mind that he didn't, a sleepy audience came awake. So did the rest of the country. Forget that he later revised the number downward to 57; reporters and editors in Wheeling would verify the number 205.[3] Joe was under way.

McCarthy had certain unusual talents. He was a solipsist, a man without moral constraints. He could lie and bully and never feel a twinge. And he had a way with alliteration in his speech, as in "the crimson clique in the State Department responsible for our loss of China."[4] Beyond these political gifts, as Rosenblatt noted, "he had cited a plausible danger—there were some Communists in our government and trade unions. In the last analysis, Joe was a creature of our times, not a creator."

Inside the Capitol, McCarthy probably wasn't as well known as his nemesis, Rosenblatt. This would soon change.

"Joe wasn't an interesting rogue but a mean guy, a college boxer," said Rosenblatt, who likened the senator to a classmate at the University of Wisconsin, a heavyweight boxer and, like McCarthy, a bully. "Joe would rather hurt an opponent than win the fight," he observed.

Having magnified a modest war record into a modest political career by posing behind a .50-caliber machine gun in the rear seat of a Marine dive bomber—hence the derisive nickname "Tailgunner Joe"—McCarthy was probably oblivious to the tangled affairs going on between the postwar United States and China. This wasn't federal subsidies for milk and cheese or funds for Wisconsin roads. It was a mess of heightened expectations, the phony suggestion of a Christianized Chinese democracy, an illusion handsomely promoted by the son of a Chinese missionary, Henry Luce, the most influential magazine publisher of the twentieth century. Most Americans fell for it, along with the illusion that the U.S. had "lost" China, thanks to *Time, Life,* and *Fortune.*

"Without Henry Luce there would have been no Joe McCarthy," said Gore Vidal, the historical novelist, perhaps pressing too far a hard kernel of truth.[5] Luce certainly provided red-hot raw material for the demagogue. Ironically, *Time* magazine would become one of McCarthy's earliest critics—having "made" him, Luce would help break him.

But much thanks to Luce, Congress was excessively generous to China's Kuomintang (Nationalist) government, led by Chiang Kai-shek. Before their total collapse in 1949, the Nationalists got $125 million from the U.S. Congress, "money that could be spent by that government for anything it wanted—no strings attached," said W. Walton Butterworth, U.S. minister in Nanking. Arms to fight the Commies? "My impression now, a couple of decades later," remarked Butterworth, "is that no military equipment ever landed on the mainland."[6] The $125 million went elsewhere.

Madame Chiang, beautiful and bright, played leading lady in the Kuomintang's pursuit of more American treasure to shore up its collapsing government. But the tap was running dry. In frustration, she called American politicians "clodhoppers" and "boors." President Truman didn't like what she said and, as usual, spoke his thoughts on the Kuomintang leaders: "They're thieves, every damned one of them. They stole $750 million out of the billions we sent to Chiang and it's invested in real estate down there in [Brazil], and some in New York."

"Controls on appropriations in those days were very loose," Rosenblatt noted. It's a sure bet some of that appropriation got kicked back to the U.S. "China Lobby" for its efforts in Washington on Chiang's behalf.

Busy in the corridors on the Hill and in the clubs around it, Rosenblatt was oblivious to China's drift into a civil war between the coalition of warlords under Chiang—portrayed by Henry Luce as the oriental answer to Thomas Jefferson—and the Communists under Mao Tse-tung. He had, however, made Joe McCarthy's acquaintance.

"Our first meeting was somewhat embarrassing," recalled Rosenblatt, already a well-established liberal. "It was breakfast in the Carroll Arms. I invited McCarthy and two or three other senators to talk about the 'non-skeds.' I was surprised he showed up. He never spoke. We behaved stiffly. But it wasn't a brush-off. He feigned concern for my problems on the Hill, offered to sponsor bills, write to the Civil Aeronautics Board, or join any other action to help the nonscheduled airlines. I figured his eagerness to help had everything to do with his eagerness to boost his reputation and win reelection. He needed help.

"There was nothing special about him, except that he was rarely alone. Usually with Roy Cohn, Jay Sourwine—a messy, unpleasant man, most aptly named—or Don Surine, a lantern-jawed, gloomy-looking ex-FBI agent. I was bothered by the characters around Joe. I always figured someone else was picking up the tabs. I had no idea he would soon become one of the most celebrated—notorious—senators. At the time, nothing special."[8]

McCarthy was then fishing for an issue to power his 1952 reelection campaign. Early in January 1950 he lunched at Washington's Colony restaurant with Father Edmund Walsh, dean of Georgetown University's foreign service school, and

William Roberts, columnist Drew Pearson's attorney. Roberts suggested the St. Lawrence Seaway. Joe said, "Not enough sex." Walsh said, "What about the Communist issue? The government is full of Communists."[9]

It clicked. One month later, Joe, the "waterboy for real-estate interests," as Rosenblatt recalled his derogatory sobriquet, had an issue to take to a GOP fund-raiser in Wheeling, West Virginia. Why had the United States "lost China"? Because Commies in the State Department were for Communist Mao and against America's ally, Chiang Kai-shek.

The timing was uncanny. "Creeping Communism" was a popular concern: Eastern Europe had fallen under Soviet hegemony; Stalin had laid a blockade on Berlin; Ethel and Julius Rosenberg had been caught spying and sentenced to execution; Alger Hiss had been caught lying about his Communist past. This had already been sufficient to ignite American hysteria. Now, on top of it, the U.S. had "lost China."

Before Joe's stir-'em-up, shake-'em-down Lincoln Day speech to West Virginia Republicans, it's unlikely that he knew any more about Patrick Jay Hurley than as a name in the newspapers, and even less about Alfred Kohlberg, sometime importer of cheap Chinese textiles, which he sold for a fortune. This would change within a month, and so would American history.

General Hurley, conqueror of homeless ex-soldiers camping in Depression-era Washington—the "Bonus Marchers"—went to China in 1944 as President Roosevelt's choice to settle the conflict between the Communists and the Nationalists. Never mind ideology. This was strategically important for ending World War II. The U.S. counted on South China as the base for launching an invasion of Japan. Only the successful use of the atomic bomb obviated that strategy.

America's soldiers on the scene, General Joseph Stilwell and Colonel Evans Carlson, were concerned that Chiang cared more about fighting Mao than about fighting Tojo. Tojo's Japanese troops were killing American soldiers in the South Pacific, and Roosevelt wanted Hurley to get the two Chinese sides together to fight Japan.

Regardless of Hurley's personality—fancy dresser, name dropper (as in "Joe" for Stalin and "Winston" for Churchill)—this may have been an impossible mission. But Hurley's limited knowledge of China and his deep concern for his own place in history didn't help the U.S. cause. "Overbearing and vindictive" is the description of Hurley from newsman Albert Ravenholt, the United Press bureau chief in Chungking, where he covered Roosevelt's emissary.[10]

Hurley did get Mao Tse-tung ("Moose Dung," as the old cowboy pronounced it) and Chiang Kai-shek ("Chanker Jack") to pose together for a UP photo. They would never get that close again. The mission gained only a short pause in China's civil war—not the Nobel Peace Prize so desired by the would-be peacemaker.[11]

Somewhat surprisingly, the incomparable American soldier-diplomat George Marshall could do no better. Assigned by President Truman to replace Hurley as peacemaker between Mao and Chiang in 1946, he, too, failed. For a man accustomed to success, it was "extremely frustrating," a major disappointment.[12] Marshall continued as secretary of state, helping to save postwar Western Europe from Communism though the use of massive American economic aid, the Marshall Plan.

"Hurley blamed his failure on State Department China experts and vowed to gain revenge," recalled Ravenholt, who spent several evenings over drinks with the ambassador after the collapse of the Chiang-Mao talks. "Hurley would get even by providing Joe McCarthy with names and details of those he accused of thwarting his mission." They included Owen Lattimore, John Davies, John Carter Vincent, John Service, and Edmund Clubb, all State Department advisors or foreign service officers who, according to Pat Hurley, wanted Mao's Commies to take over China. Clubb, a former University of Washington student of China, was chief of the department's China desk. Eventually Hurley would lay the same accusation against General Stilwell, a conservative Republican who was contemptuous of the Kuomintang's corruption and its unwillingness to fight the Japanese.[13]

In March 1945, while Hurley seethed and talked of betrayal, agents of the Office of Strategic Services (OSS) raided the Manhattan offices of *Amerasia,* an obscure fortnightly magazine of a pro-Communist persuasion, where they found State Department documents marked "confidential" or "secret." They called the FBI.

One of these documents, a report on Thailand, had run nearly verbatim in *Amerasia's* January 26 issue. The editor hadn't even called for a rewrite. He was Phillip Jaffe, a Communist sympathizer, if not a party member, a supporter of Joseph Stalin, and a booster of Mao Tse-tung.

Thus the nation got "Amerasia," the spy case that wouldn't die, despite a grand jury investigation based on FBI wiretaps, a House of Representatives probe of the State Department (whence came the leaked documents), and a Senate investigation under the conservative—nay, patrician—Democrat Millard Tydings of Maryland. It would, in a short time, cost Tydings his political career.

None of the investigations found evidence of espionage. Jaffe and an aide were eventually indicted for conspiracy to steal government documents. Five others walked, including John Service, ex-aide to Hurley, who had fired him for being critical of Chiang and too chummy with Chinese Commies.[14] Service may have dished off the documents to get even with Hurley, whom he regarded as ignorant or slightly cracked.

This was hot stuff for conspiracy theorists. In the aftermath of the *Amerasia* affair, William Randolph Hearst's *New York Journal-American* headlined, "Sensational Proof Communists Had Access to Confidential Files." The Hearst chain's other New York entry, the *Mirror,* bannered, "More Arrests Forecast in Spy Hunt." None were made.

In fact, the two indictments, the political equivalents of jay-walking tickets, looked fishy. Had the Truman administration pulled grand jury strings to spare itself embarrassment? There was evidence of a fix of federal prosecutors by Tommy Corcoran, a veteran Democratic wheeler-dealer. He was an operator who could make promises and call in debts. He was also an officer in a company formed to channel U.S. aid to Chinese nationalists.[15]

Corcoran's inside game may have been played with the connivance of Chiang Kai-shek. Given a trial, two certain witnesses would have been Stilwell and Service. Released from a gag order, Stilwell could have spilled the beans on Kuomintang corruption. Service could have told how Chiang slipped around on his beautiful wife—"Mrs. Shek" as Hurley called the imperious madame.[16] The Chiangs had been pumped as Asia's model couple, an oriental Tracy and Hepburn, role setters for an up-and-coming democracy.

Exposure of Chiang's infidelity and misuse of American money would have cost the Kuomintang congressional appropriations, millions of which, wrote Drew Pearson, vanished into private bank accounts.[17] Chiang and his madame never lacked the cash for high living. Equally flush was Alfred Kohlberg's China Lobby. Kohlberg, Senator Wayne Morse alleged, got money from the U.S. Treasury, kicked back through Chiang.[18] Kohlberg was a major force on Capitol Hill who had his way with parts of the American press, most conspicuously the Hearst and Scripps-Howard newspaper chains and the *Chicago Tribune.*

Leftovers from Father Coughlin's Christian Front of the 1930s were Kohlberg's top aides. They included Robert Harris, one-time Coughlin financial advisor; Joseph Kamp, a pro-Nazi propagandist; and William Goodwin, the Christian Front candidate for mayor of New York in 1941, now a $30,000-a-year flack for Chiang in Washington.[19]

From his prewar anti-fascist organizational work in New York City, Rosenblatt had acquired more than a passing acquaintance with the Manhattan gang Coughlin left to Kohlberg. "Kamp was an associate of Allen Zoll, the pro-Nazi agent in pursuit of actress Jenny Parmenter's letters from her lover, George Earle, FDR's pal and ambassador to Bulgaria. Goodwin ran the Christian Front's stronghold in New York City's Queens borough," he said. Subsequently, Kohlberg made a fancy Chinese restaurant on Connecticut Avenue a postwar watering hole and dining hall for the China Lobby. Rosenblatt, an observer, described the food as excellent.

A few weeks after McCarthy's Wheeling speech, Kohlberg, already well connected on Capitol Hill, called for a meeting with Joe and Hurley. They had dinner at the more public Mayflower Hotel in Washington, where the businessman-lobbyist and the ex-diplomat related "the full story of the China sell-out to the anti-Communist senator."[20] Hurley would have his vengeance.

McCarthy's accusations against the State Department could "be traced to Hurley's charges and *Plain Talk*," wrote Ross Koen in his book *The China Lobby in American Politics.*[21] *Plain Talk* was the China Lobby's house organ. Barbara Tuchman put it more forcefully in her epic account *Stilwell and the American Experience in China:* "Hurley opened the journey to the tawdry reign of terror soon to be imposed with such astonishing ease by Senator Joe McCarthy."[22]

By the spring of 1950, with startling speed, McCarthy had Americans under a spell and, in the Senate, a coterie of "Little Joes": Styles Bridges, Owen Brewster, Homer Capehart, Harry P. Cain, Kenneth Wherry, and, most importantly, Bob Taft, "Mr. Conservative." They all seemed to be cheering, "Go, Joe, Go!" Taft declared, "If one case doesn't work out, bring up another."[23]

And so McCarthy did: Phillip Jessup, a State Department consultant, "a man with an affinity for Communist causes"; John Service, "Russia's top espionage agent in the State Department"; and Owen Lattimore, China scholar and political naif.[24] Lattimore had once called the 1937 Moscow show trials of Stalin's enemies—inspiration for Arthur Koestler's dramatization *Darkness at Noon*—"democracy in action."[25] As the columnist Joe Alsop sighed, he was "a man of great learning and befuddled politics."[26] McCarthy declaimed, "The corpse of China bears mute evidence of how valuable the Services, Jessups, and Lattimores have been to Russia."[27]

There was at least one critical reaction. "When I read what McCarthy said about Lattimore, I became very emotional, perhaps determined to do something to right a wrong," said Maurice Rosenblatt. And in time, so he would.

3 | The "McCarthy" Elections, 1950 and 1952

REPUBLICANS HAD A TICKET TO RIDE and a national figure to carry the banner in the next two general elections. In most parts of the nation by 1950 the Communist Party was a phantom, a diminished threat to the democracy not much greater than the Ku Klux Klan. But as portrayed by Joe McCarthy and the "Little Joes," it was a phantom "boring from within"—red-hot campaign ammunition to use against Democrats.

Indeed, by February 1950 a political diagnostician might have said that the country was running a high fever. McCarthy had given the fever a name: "McCarthyism." You could measure it by newspaper headlines: "Plan Roundup of 4,000 Reds," "Soviets Detonate Atom Bomb" (1949), "Red Army Conquers China," "Klaus Fuchs Atom Spy for Soviets," "Alger Hiss Guilty!" of lying about passing secret documents to a confessed Communist.[1] And all of this happening under a Democratic administration. It was a ticket to ride.

"After the Wheeling speech, the Senate nobody [McCarthy] quickly became a national figure," said Maurice Rosenblatt. "Initially, there was little press notice. Then I began to realize that he could get ink. It came one day in the corridor of the old Senate Office Building. I heard a great commotion, a crowd of people. Someone shouted, 'Joe is going to the [Senate] floor.' Sure enough, and followed by a flock of reporters. Wherever he went, he drew a crowd."

Among political sophisticates, there was concern over a switch in global strategy from "communist containment" to "preventive war," as advocated by Senator Harry Cain of Washington State, among others. Norman Cousins, editor of the *Saturday Review of Literature*, wired Marshall Field, the newspaper publisher, of Averill Harriman's concern over "increasing forces pushing for preventive war." Cousins called for a meeting to discuss strategy at the home of Telford Taylor, a New Deal lawyer and the United States' chief prosecutor at the Nuremberg war crimes trials, in early October 1950. "Senate races are critical," he said.[2]

The call was prescient, but a winning Democratic strategy never materialized. With McCarthy out front, campaigning in a dozen states, Republicans won 52 percent of the 1950 general election votes, shrinking the Senate Democratic majority from twelve votes to two, and the House majority from seventeen to twelve.[3] Joe took personal delight in smears against Senate majority leader Scott Lucas and Maryland's conservative Democratic senator, Millard Tydings. Through his aide Jean Kerr, he micro-managed the campaign against Tydings.

Lucas had fatally misjudged McCarthy. In May he allowed that Joe "had made so many charges without proof, people are not paying attention any longer; [McCarthy] will have very little effect on the coming elections." Wrong. Lucas lost his seat. So did Tydings, Pennsylvania's Senator Francis Meyers, and three other Senate Democrats.[4]

"Lucas provided the whitewash when I charged there were Communists in high places in government," said McCarthy in a full-service campaign speech. "McMahon [Senator Brian] brought the bucket, Tydings the brush." Absent Joe, Lucas might have survived payoff scandals in the Cook County Democratic machine to win reelection. He didn't.

"We were overwhelmed," said Rosenblatt, whose new organization, the National Committee for an Effective Congress, had played a critical role in the 1948 election of six new members of the Senate. But that was then; this was two years later, with a new national mood and, as of June, a war in Korea. "McCarthy's group was stronger and had great access to the press," he remarked. "Joe's use of the press was an embarrassment to the whole journalism profession."[5]

McCarthy went way below the belt to get Tydings, whose subcommittee had investigated the *Amerasia* case and found

McCarthy's (and indirectly Pat Hurley's) charges of a Communist conspiracy inside the State Department to be a "hoax and a fraud."[6] Joe was unforgiving. His aides circulated a phony composite photo showing the Maryland patrician posed alongside Earl Browder, the Stalinist Communist Party USA leader. The *New York Times,* among other publications, carried a print of the false picture on November 12 that year. In fact, if not in this faked photo, Tydings and Browder had about as much in common as Dick Nixon and Groucho Marx.

"Tydings had a pedigree and property, a Silver Star decoration for heroism in World War I—he was the squire of Havre de Grace, an opponent of the New Deal," in Rosenblatt's description. No matter to Joe McCarthy. This was a get-even campaign engineered by Joe for Tydings's "whitewash" of "Communists in government," most of them initially targeted by Pat Hurley and his man in Washington, Alfred Kohlberg.

In a Senate floor speech, McCarthy charged that "as a result of the so-called investigation [by Tydings's subcommittee] of the State Department, disloyal persons were shielded from exposure, with the ultimate result that Communist subversion in the government was whitewashed."

The whitewash charge and the faked photo were carried in what Rosenblatt called "the rawest piece of campaign literature ever made," a four-page tabloid labeling Secretary of State Dean Acheson "pro-Communist."

John Marshall Butler's (and McCarthy's) victory over Tydings, according to Joe, "was a great election victory for the people of Maryland and of the nation, a well-deserved defeat for Tydings." Besides, said Joe, Butler ran "an honest, clean campaign." In fact, the campaign against Tydings was dirty enough to merit a Senate subcommittee investigation, which indeed called it questionable but nevertheless allowed Butler to keep his Senate seat.

It was a turning point for Joe—and the nation, Rosenblatt suggested: "McCarthy takes on Millard Tydings—a war hero, senior Democrat, a really important man in the Senate. Suddenly he's brought down. By who? Joe McCarthy. We realize Joe is not just another senator, but a power. You take a nobody—like Joe. He fights. He stays up. All of a sudden you say he's worth watching. It was McCarthy's cumulative power from staying in the ring."

There was a bizarre and unresolved aspect to that now nearly forgotten campaign. McCarthy's designated Maryland hit man was Don Surine, the lapsed FBI agent, a regular along with Joe come evenings in the basement bar of the Carroll Arms. Rosenblatt, who observed him, said, "Surine could have come out of a Dostoyevsky novel, skinny, lantern-jawed, hair disheveled. I never knew when Surine might sneak up behind me and put a knife in my back. But this was McCarthy's man."

Tydings accused the ex-Fed of "Chicago gangland tactics" in his snatch of a Butler campaign aide, William Fedder, and their subsequent six-hour midnight ride around Baltimore. Surine's apparent aim was to secure a letter from Fedder that showed Butler in violation of Maryland campaign laws. Fedder claimed he feared for his life. Surine said no, he had made no threats. The facts of this affair were never made clear.[7]

The investigating subcommittee, with Democrats in the majority, denounced Butler's campaign as "a despicable, back-street type" but stopped short of recommending that he be sent back to Baltimore, expelled from the Senate chamber.[8] The hearing did nothing to arrest McCarthyism or its namesake. On the contrary: the fallout of publicity may have increased its momentum.

Out West, in California, Representative Richard Nixon capitalized on his apparent unmasking of Alger Hiss as a card-carrying Commie to defeat the remarkable Helen Gahagan Douglas for a Senate seat. Mrs. Douglas was an intellect, a beauty, an actress, the wife of actor Melvyn Douglas, and a hand-holding Capitol Hill companion to Lyndon Johnson, a fellow member of Congress.[9] This was Rosenblatt's pre-election summary of that historic California contest and prospects for a new, more enlightened Far Eastern (China) policy, as he wrote it to Agriculture Secretary Charles Brannan in June 1950: "Nixon's chances in California are better than ever. Should he prevail, the Senate will have a cold, adroit inquisitor, a methodical and calculating strategist whose talent for evil far outweighs any of Joe McCarthy's demagogic antics." Maurice figured Nixon would be more attached to the Kuomintang than was McCarthy.[10]

That assessment was nearly pitch perfect, but recall that in June 1950 McCarthy was just getting warmed up and, with the prodding of the China Lobby, had already so poisoned the political atmosphere that hope for a "Titoist" China (a Communist government detached from the Soviet Union) was slim to none. Rosenblatt noted: "No statesman or citizen dares explore approaches to a new Far Eastern policy for fear of being [called] a part of a sinister Communist cabal."[11] That fear would prevail—irony of ironies—for two decades, until President Nixon himself traveled to "Red China" and commenced normal Sino-American relations.

Elsewhere out West, in Washington State, where the Communist Party had considerable influence inside the Democratic Party in the 1930s, the Commie phantom had legs. There was fact to back the insinuations of Red baiters.

One of the more powerful Democrats, Senator Warren Magnuson, seemed vulnerable to McCarthyite charges. After all, he had sought and secured Communist Party support in his first run for Congress. Accordingly, Albert Canwell, now a household name in the Northwest, sought the GOP nomination to oppose Magnuson. He had run a state legislative committee investigation of Communists on the University of Washington faculty. Three professors lost their jobs. Canwell's slogan: "Let's get the Reds out of government and the government out of the Red."[12] Alas for him, the campus Commie hunter lost the nomination to a conservative Seattle businessman. But the force of the Communist issue was undiminished.

Even where Joe didn't intervene directly, McCarthyism—guilt by association—filled his absence. In one example, the *Seattle Times* acknowledged that although Magnuson was not guilty of outright subversion, he was "guilty of giving protection to leaders of the Communist line of thought in the state over the years."

Magnuson barely won the 1950 election, much thanks to his considerable support from the state's business community and McCarthy's indifference to his opponent's campaign. "Maggie" could, as they say, bring home the bacon, in this case hydro-electric dams, military contracts (Boeing's B-17), roads, bridges, welfare, and military bases. Most curious: despite the closeness of this race, Magnuson did not campaign on his own role in purging Communists and "security risks" from the nation's waterfronts. Instead, he stayed silent, perhaps from embarrassment or even remorse.

Owen Brewster, the Maine senator and GOP Senate campaign chairman, declared McCarthy "decisive" in the party's eight election victories, then lamented that the Red baiter hadn't been used in other states (Washington?). Better use of Joe, said Brewster, would have gained the GOP control of the Senate.[13]

But wait. Another national election was two years hence, and the Communist issue and its major player remained toxic. If anything, the Red scare and the Republicans' use of it ran even stronger in the fall of 1952. Consider a national sample from the 1952 election campaigns. In West Virginia, Revercomb Chapman charged that Senator Harley Kilgore had "aided and appeased Communist causes" and had a record of "continuous sympathy with Communist thinkers." In Maryland, Republican J. Glenn Beall bemoaned the "nation's headlong plunge down the paths of precepts dictated by the teaching of Karl Marx." In Montana, Democratic candidate Mike Mansfield, "a captive of the Truman-Acheson gang[,] helped give China to the Reds." McCarthy was said to have a violent hatred of Mansfield, one of the nation's most distinguished public officials, and probably had a hand in this campaign. Running for reelection to the Senate in Washington State, Harry Cain accused his opponent, Henry Jackson, of "Communist mollycoddling."[14]

In the face of this anti-Commie fever, Robert Sherwood, the playwright, a board member of the National Committee for an Effective Congress, gave an upbeat assessment of liberal prospects a month before the elections. "McCarthyism hasn't killed civil liberties and academic freedom—it only threatens," he said.

"This [election] is the hour of counterattack. The results will show if we can be free of the Joe McCarthy [Senate] bloc."[15] Accordingly, his organization supported Democratic candidates Henry Jackson, Dennis Chavez, William Benton, and Mike Mansfield, all elected to the Senate in 1952. Overall, however, election results were mixed.

Breezing to reelection in Wisconsin, McCarthy took time off the 1952 campaign trail in October for a trip from Milwaukee to Minot, North Dakota, to address the Young Republican Club and to hunt ducks. His party of seven included former Minnesota Congressman Elmer Ryan and John Matchette, a sometime Pan-American Airlines pilot and a pal of Maurice Rosenblatt's. They flew west in a DC-3 owned by the boss of Evinrude Outboard Motors. Matchette got aboard courtesy of his friend Al Harvey, who introduced him to McCarthy.

"Al said you don't care much for my viewpoints," said McCarthy. "But Al said you are not dangerous."

"I wish I could say the same about you," Matchette replied.

"With that, McCarthy laughed out loud, a big strong Irish laugh," Matchette recalled. "I was welcomed to the party. Joe was a blustery, hail-fellow-well-met, quite charming when he wanted to be, which was most of the time, being a politician. He didn't play the big shot. He laughed at himself. I think he was sort of ambivalent. He gave a different impression on television in the Army-McCarthy hearings."[16]

Young Republicans scared ducks up from the Souris River to within range of the shooters, "but McCarthy was a terrible shot. He kept missing, and he wasn't drinking. He had a speech to make that night," said Matchette. To retrieve the fowls felled by those who could shoot straight, McCarthy waded into the icy river, taking water down his boots. Back ashore, he lay on his back, raised his legs, allowing the water to pour down, and laughed. Good-time Joe.

The senator's speech that evening attacked Phillip Jessup, the State Department consultant. "He didn't call him a Communist," said Matchette. "If he had, I might have admired him. Instead he said, 'If it looks like a skunk, walks like a skunk, smells like a skunk, it must be a skunk.'" You got the point about Jessup by indirection, as Matchette noted to Elmer Ryan, Joe's close ally. "Why, Jessup isn't a Communist," said Ryan. "He's a pinko."[17]

McCarthy, playing the good-time Joe, may not have been aware of a plot behind the scenes to oust him in the Republican primary election. Pushed by William Hurley (no kin to Patrick Hurley), chief of the Wisconsin State Radio network, the aim was to talk General Douglas MacArthur, a native of the state, into running in the Republican primary. Hurley and his friends were convinced that the American military hero would defeat McCarthy and continue to serve the nation from his Senate pulpit.

It didn't work. MacArthur wanted to run on the 1952 GOP ticket either as Senator Robert Taft's vice presidential nominee or as the presidential candidate himself. Attempts by Hurley and others to talk the general into the Senate race failed. MacArthur underestimated the political appeal of his former aide, General Dwight Eisenhower, whom he did not like. Surprise—a majority of the delegates to the Republican convention in Chicago that year did "Like Ike," a first ballot winner. MacArthur faded away to retirement in Manhattan's Waldorf Astoria Hotel.[18]

Free at home from a formidable campaign, Joe hit the road again to help other Republican candidates, perhaps none more important than Harry P. Cain, a "Little Joe," a strident reactionary seeking reelection to another Senate term from Washington State. He faced Representative Henry M. "Scoop" Jackson, a second-generation Scandinavian American and a straightforward Northwestern progressive. Joe came to Seattle to help. The upshot in this otherwise dreary election year was a burst of political comedy.

The Seattle Press Club arranged a debate between McCarthy and the state's leading stand-up comic, Lieutenant Governor Victor A. Meyers, a former bandleader turned all-time showman. (Sample from the showdown: Q— "Vic, how do you stand on the Communist issue?" A— "Of course, my boy, I'm all right on that one. Next question.") A bully in the Senate, Joe didn't like being the target of laughter, which came in small gales at the Press Club face-off. He stalked out of the club in anger for the studios of KING-TV, to give a televised address.[19]

More frustration. The studio turned him away; no air time for Joe, because of his refusal to strike parts of his prepared speech that company attorneys considered libelous. Never mind. Hearst's *Seattle Post-Intelligencer* took a copy of his speech and ran it verbatim in morning editions, including a paragraph alleging that two members of columnist Drew Pearson's staff were ex-Commies.

And Joe got word out through the ever-eager press that Jackson was "soft on Communism." Taking the cue, Seattle and Spokane newspapers attacked Jackson and Hugh B. Mitchell, Democratic candidate for governor, for their sponsorship of the Columbia Valley Authority. It would have been the Northwest's counterpart to the Tennessee Valley Authority—federal management of the river and its critical hydroelectric generators. The papers called it "Communistic socialistic" and, more poetically, "Communism on the Columbia."[20] The private power companies, Puget Power, Portland Gas and Electric, Idaho Power, Washington Water Power, loved those editorials, if in fact they did not write them.

Election results were split. Mitchell lost the primary election, victim of the "soft on Communism" charge. Jackson won. Both went on to distinguished careers, Mitchell as a businessman, Jackson as a Senate stalwart on behalf of national defense and environmental protection.

Thanks to McCarthy, the 1952 election left the Senate with forty-eight Republicans and forty-seven Democrats, together with Republican President Dwight Eisenhower—who refused to denounce his party's prime demagogue—and Vice President Richard Nixon, who had helped inspire him. It would move Joe McCarthy to chairman of the Senate Permanent Subcommittee on Investigations, the forum that would give the United States "McCarthyism."

It seems odd that McCarthy, who never lacked for money or whiskey, in Rosenblatt's observation, steered clear of the Senate race in Massachusetts—Republican Henry Cabot Lodge against the young war hero, Representative John F. Kennedy. Maurice said the answer to that riddle was easy: father Joe Kennedy intervened on behalf of son Jack with a contribution to McCarthy on the order of $10,000. Accordingly, Joe kept his distance from the liberal Jack.

The father went further in nurturing son Jack's campaign. To secure support from organized labor, Joe Kennedy brought in Gardner Jackson, a friend of Rosenblatt's from his New York days with close ties to the AFL-CIO. Jackson met with Kennedy and his aide, Kenny O'Donnell, in the congressman's Beacon Hill apartment in Boston. Rosenblatt relayed the scene that followed from Gardner Jackson's stunning description:

"They briefly discussed labor support. Jackson had come prepared with the draft of a speech for Jack to deliver to a labor rally. While he was reading the draft Joe Kennedy walked into the room. He stayed silent for a few minutes, listening. Suddenly he jumped up from a chair, grabbed the draft paper, and tossed it across the room.

"'You and your sheenie friends are going to beat my son!' he shouted, stalking out of the apartment. There was dead silence. Finally Jackson said, 'Jack, I don't understand your father. I just don't understand. He's got the whole thing wrong.' I think Joe was reacting to what he saw as a shift by his son to the left wing.

"Finally, Jack responded, telling Jackson, 'Put it down to pride of family, Gardner. Love of family.' Despite the outburst on Beacon Hill, Jackson kept Kennedy in contact with Eastern labor unions while Joe Miller, the Seattle newshawk turned Washington lobbyist, did much the same out West."[21]

The rest is history. Kennedy won the Senate seat and eight years later was nominated by the Democratic Party and elected president. He never resolved his ambivalent feelings about Joe McCarthy. Privately, he must have regarded Joe as a boor, in contrast to his own charm and humor. In public, and for the record, Kennedy was silent, quite possibly in deference to his father.[22]

Apart from the legitimate fear of Communism and the possibility of its subversion of government, McCarthy had tapped a partisan current already running strong in these two general elections. Republicans wanted more than revenge for the loss of the White House to Harry Truman. They aimed for a drastic reversal of U.S. internationalist foreign policy. Here, too, Joe played a role.

Led by Senator Robert Taft of Ohio, with support from Senators Bourke Hickenlooper, William Langer, and William Knowland on the Foreign Relations Committee, neo-isolationists demanded repudiation of the "secret agreements" President Roosevelt had made in his meetings with Joseph Stalin at Yalta near the end of World War II. Those agreements had given the Soviets de facto control of Eastern Europe. The neo-isolationists wanted to "free" those satellite states—never saying exactly how they would go about this potential starter for World War III.

In 1952, with the election of a Republican-controlled House, a nearly equally divided Senate, and a GOP president, the time looked ripe to strike against the deals at Yalta. But when Ike balked (Secretary of State John Dulles said there were no secret deals) and Senator Lyndon Johnson brought Democrats onto the president's side, the matter was dropped—but for lack of votes, not passion.[23] McCarthy maintained a leading role, again, as in Maryland, playing the low road.

Passion carried over into a hot skirmish about the selection of Charles Bohlen, an advisor to Roosevelt at Yalta, as U.S. ambassador to Moscow. On the Senate floor McCarthy claimed to have seen Bohlen's sealed FBI file and that it contained damaging information about the diplomat's "family life." That was 1952 code for homosexuality, and the accusation was too wild even for the vengeful Taft. Bohlen got confirmed. I. F. Stone, in his March 1953 newsletter, summed up the episode as having been carried out by "a coalition of the simple-minded and the sinister in the fight against Bohlen."[24]

Isolationists would also fail to move from the Congress a constitutional amendment that would have forced the president to gain approval from Congress and from state legislatures in order to consummate any international compact. The "Bricker Amendment," creature of Senator John Bricker of Ohio, one of the Taft cadre favoring American withdrawal from most of the world, was fought over for years, finally dying a protracted death. Eisenhower called it "a stupid, blind violation of the Constitution by stupid, blind isolationists."[25]

McCarthy played no significant role in the constitutional battle. He had a larger and more timely agenda: a search-and-destroy mission on behalf of anti-Communism, or anything that seemed in his view to approach it, regardless of international boundaries.

Riding high after the 1950 and 1952 elections, McCarthy, the new chairman of the Subcommittee on Investigations, pushed his Red raids beyond U.S. borders. In early 1953 he dispatched his committee's counsel, Roy Cohn, and its investigator, G. David Schine, to Europe to seek out and ban subversive books in libraries run by the U.S. Information Agency.

Save for his close relationship with Roy Cohn, Schine was an odd selection for an intellectual gumshoe—or for that matter, any kind of gumshoe. A rich kid, son of a hotel magnate, he flashed it at Harvard, where he was served by a personal valet and tooled around Cambridge in a black convertible.[26] He served on the committee without pay, according to Ruth Young Watt, the investigation committee's chief clerk and master of the payroll; he was "just a consultant on his own."[27] At one point, Schine actually proposed to spread democracy in Asia by distributing pictures of pinup girls and establishing "Elks Clubs in Pakistan."[28]

The library hit list uncovered by Cohn and Schine included the papers of General Joseph Stillwell, the *New Republic* and *Nation* magazines, and books by Agnes Smedley, a reporter friendly with Chinese Communists. Back home, McCarthy claimed his sleuths had found "thirty thousand to forty thousand" books by Communists and fellow travelers in U.S.-sponsored libraries.[29] These included *The Maltese Falcon* and *The Thin Man*, by Dashiel Hammett, a sometime party member whose well-written books had everything to do with vicarious entertainment—both made excellent films—and nothing to do with ideology. Even more sinisterly, the dynamic duo cited the absence of anti-Communist magazines, most conspicuously the *American Legion Monthly*. *Newsweek* and Luce's pro-Kuomintang, anti-Commie *Time*, apparently, were insufficient.

Laugh now, but this nonsense captured more press ink than the Rose Bowl, the World Series, and General Motors' new line of zoom-finned automobiles, not all of it spilled by Hearst and the *Tribune*. It also inspired a catch line of those times: "So long, see you tomorrow—come Cohn or come Schine."

McCarthy's ideological press allies aside, a question remains about the lack of skepticism (never mind cynicism) the press showed toward him. It was a faint rationalization to think, What the hell, maybe some of his charges are factually true; deep down we're really doing a good service to the country even if we're doing a disservice to our profession.

Alas, the record shows that McCarthy had little success, if any, in uncovering actual American subversives. This does not diminish his triumph, if that's the word for it, in critically exaggerating a climate of fear and distrust in the United States. Its place in American history endures.

4 McCarthyism

IT MAY BE IMPOSSIBLE to transmit to later generations how Joe McCarthy—that is, McCarthyism—chilled dissent in our society. "What are you, some kind of Communist?" one might ask in response to an off-center comment, say, a sympathetic word about a movie star tagged with the heresy. In the early 1950s that was a warning, not a joke. Once tagged, the victim was stuck, frequently out of a job, unable to prove his or her innocence. Social scientists labeled those coming of age in the 1950s the "silent generation." They were quiet, and not without reason—self-preservation.

A parable in the *New Yorker* on March 26, 1953, captured the essential McCarthyism: "A squirrel spots a rabbit digging furiously into the earth. Puzzled, he inquires as to why. The rabbit explains that Joe McCarthy is going to investigate all antelopes, so you, pal, should go climb the highest tree. 'You're crazy! I'm no antelope.' To which the rabbit replies, 'Of course not, nor am I, but I'm digging anyway. How can I prove that I'm not an antelope?' " Was it mere coincidence that Franz Kafka, a somewhat obscure middle-European writer of tales about hapless individuals snared in inexplicable traps, suddenly surged to popularity in U.S. academic circles in the early 1950s?

After Communist North Korea invaded South Korea in June 1950, anti-Communism—McCarthy's sometimes wild, usually unsubstantiated charges notwithstanding—gained an increased measure of respectability. Many politically sophisticated people saw the action as a brute extension of Kremlin power. "Red" China was regarded as a Kremlin satellite, à la Poland. Politically, of course, the Korean War and the "loss" of China were blights on the Democratic administration.

Given the political atmosphere, it wasn't much of a stretch from McCarthy to McCarthyism. For instance, on August 6, 1950, at the Astor Hotel in New York City, McCarthy addressed the Veterans of Foreign Wars (VFW) convention, a friendly crowd that shouted, "Give those Reds hell" and "McCarthy for president!" Joe tossed them a warm-up pitch of alleged treason: the State Department's Phillip Jessup "belongs to or was affiliated with not one, not two, but with five Communist Party fronts." Later: "You can't fight this State Department with a lace handkerchief." And finally: "I will not be intimidated by the *Daily Worker* or the *New York Post*," the latter a liberal, not a Communist, newspaper. Joe made a career of feasting on this missing distinction.[1]

The effect of McCarthy's speech on the veterans' organization may be likened to that of a drop of acid on litmus paper. McCarthyism spread. The VFW subsequently launched its own hunt for Reds in several local organizations around the nation. Suspects were to be turned over to the FBI to determine their "loyalty." As one Kansas chapter stated the case, "We are fulfilling our obligation as loyal Americans."[2] The toll of innocent victims from these ideological vigilantes will never be known.

The net of McCarthyism fell heavily on figures in the entertainment business. By 1950, *Red Channels: The Report on Communist Influences in Radio and Television,* a for-profit newsletter founded in 1947 by former FBI agent Theodore Kirkpatrick, had become a bible for the ever sensitive networks and advertising agencies. Woe to the hapless victim named—just named, no evidence needed—by this media creature of the times.

One such, the poet and anthologist Louis Untermeyer, had just joined Dorothy Kilgallen and Arlene Francis on the panel of *What's My Line,* a popular TV quiz program. CBS ran the weekly show, and mail began pouring into its offices when *Red Channels* tagged Untermeyer as affiliated with something called the "Anti-Fascist Refugee Committee," one of about ninety organizations listed by the U.S. attorney general as at least suspected of being un-American. Following the flood of anti-Untermeyer mail, the Catholic War Veterans Committee began placing stickers in drugstore windows that read, "Stop Stopette until Stopette

Stops Untermeyer." Stopette was an underarm deodorant, and its manufacturer, a sponsor of *What's My Line*. The company complied. Untermeyer was dumped, to be replaced by Bennett Cerf, a book publisher.

Thereafter the well-shaken CBS required its employees to take a "loyalty oath" and cleared its TV guests through *Red Channels*. Some didn't make the publication's grade of real Americanism—among others, symphony conductor Leonard Bernstein, actress Judy Holliday, writer Abe Burrows, singer Harry Belafonte, actress Uta Hagen, and Gypsy Rose Lee, the veteran stripteaser.[3]

In retrospect, it might almost seem as if Joe McCarthy invented anti-Communism as well as giving it his name. But credit belongs elsewhere, and not only to the Washington State Legislature, which beat the senator to the hunt for Communists with an investigation of the University of Washington faculty. President Truman himself set the stage for "guilt by association"—later a hallmark of McCarthyism—when, under right-wing pressure and alarmed by the *Amerasia* case, he instigated loyalty oaths for federal employees. Implicit in his call for oaths was the threat of internal subversion.

Under executive order 9835, dated March 27, 1947, Truman created "loyalty boards," and he told Attorney General Tom Clark to prepare a list of subversive organizations "after appropriate investigation and determination." Loyalty boards could decree government workers guilty of "sympathetic association" with such organizations.[4]

Nearly one hundred organizations, beginning with the Communist Party and an anti-Semitic group known as the Silver Shirts, modeled on Hitler's Brown Shirts, wound up on this de facto black list.[5] (Red, a shipmate in the engine room of the SS *Aleutian*, told me this tale about the Silver Shirts in Depression-era Seattle: "I was shivering in the cold rain on Skid Road when a sailor I'd known on the [SS] *Baranof* came up and said, 'Red, time you joined up with the Silver Shirts, an outfit that's going to take care of the Jews and get us jobs.' I already had a Communist Party card, but what the hell? I was cold. I said, 'Sure, I'll join. Where's the shirt?'")

Other black-listed organizations included Veterans of the Abraham Lincoln Brigade (Americans who had volunteered and fought for Spain's Republican government in the Spanish Civil War of 1936–39), the German-American Bund, the American League Against War and Fascism, the Citizens Committee for Harry Bridges (a West Coast longshoremen's union leader accused of Communism), the Commonwealth College of Mena, Arkansas, the Socialist Workers Party (pro-Trotsky, anti-Stalin), the Industrial Workers of the World ("Wobblies"), and the Washington (State) Commonwealth Federation.[6] In short, Truman gave America the loyalty boards, his attorney general wrote the black list, and McCarthyism gave them both political wings.

The FBI's blacklist of suspected Communists or sympathizers was a worker's curse. A modest example is that of Del Castle, a retired Seattle longshoreman and former Communist Party member. Castle joined the party in 1935, the pit of the Great Depression, also dropping out of the University of Washington for lack of money. Three successive postwar jobs in Seattle lasted about thirty days each before FBI agents notified Castle's employers of his connection to the blacklist. Each time he was fired. To earn a living he went "underground" and found work in California. He lingered in the Communist Party until 1957, after Soviet tanks had destroyed a democratic revolution in Hungary. The party, he said, was by then being run by "democratic centralism," in his view a two-bit term for dictatorship from the top. It was "essentially nondemocratic—a hell of a lot of bureaucratic domination." Eventually he got back to Seattle, a longshore job, and a pension. The road had been rough.[7]

Truman, before his death, conceded in private conversations that his loyalty program had been a mistake, and yes, he said, "it was terrible."[8] By 1951 three million federal employees had been investigated and cleared, and 212 dismissed for questionable loyalty. None would be indicted for espionage. Truman's aide Clark Clifford called the program "a response to the temper of the times." Later, in an interview, he said "it was a political problem—Truman was going to run for reelection in 1948 and that was it."[9]

Too often, as a remarkable document published by the California State Senate Subcommittee on Un-American Activities reported, organizations on the attorney general's list were confused with "extremely liberal groups."[10] These groups, "unjustly accused of being Communist controlled," included the American Friends Service Committee (Quakers), Americans for Democratic Action (stridently anti-Communist), United World Federalists, "and others."

The overwhelming zeal to catch and persecute heretics— Communists or anyone suspected of the slightest sympathy with them—could be likened to using a pile driver to crack a walnut. Collateral damage from this overkill has never been calculated, but anyone who lived through it knows that the ratio of innocent victims to actual Communists or sympathizers was enormous. The hunt was out of control, and worse, due legal process was discarded. Once connected to a "subversive" organization, employees were guilty until they proved their innocence. It took years for the federal courts to unravel this breach of American rights, meager consolation to a lot of employees who lost jobs or, worse, their means of livelihood. Among the latter were nearly four thousand maritime workers, seamen, and longshoremen.[11]

Although it falls under the rubric of "McCarthyism," the purge of seamen was initiated by Truman, with help from, of all people, Senator Warren Magnuson of Washington State, a hero to waterfront workers. The purge preceded the full force of McCarthy's anti-Communism and attracted far less attention. It was quick, clean, and brutal. Irv Hoff, administrative aide to Magnuson, recalled its genesis in July 1950: "Magnuson talked to President Truman (a poker-playing companion) about seaport security. There was fear that a nuclear device could be placed aboard a vessel and sneaked into one of our harbors. Truman said, 'Put in a bill.' He did, and seven days after introduction it passed the Congress and was signed into law." It gave the Coast Guard authority to inspect all incoming vessels, as Hoff recalled.[12]

What Hoff could not recall about the "Magnuson Act" was another provision that allowed the Coast Guard to yank the

U.S. Merchant Marine Document—a seaman's de facto and de jure work permit—from any seaman connected with one of the "subversive" organizations listed by the U.S. attorney general. Innocents, along with card-carrying Communist Party members, went out with the purge.

Some, like George Rogers of the Marine Cooks and Stewards Union, were active anti-Communists. No matter. Rogers had allowed his house to be used for a fundraiser on behalf of Henry Wallace's Progressive Party and had bought a raffle ticket from the Northwest Labor School, a left-wing organization cited by the attorney general. Thus Rogers was ruled a "security risk." The Coast Guard revoked his Merchant Marine Document—his seaman's passport.

The purge ended in the mid-1950s with a ruling by the Ninth Circuit Court of Appeals that the Coast Guard had to afford suspect seamen their rights to confront hostile witnesses and have access to the evidence against them—in short, American civil rights. It came too late for a majority of those seamen left on the beach, victims of a sorry, mostly ignored episode in the Red scare bearing the name of Joe McCarthy.[13]

McCarthy, yes. But Warren Magnuson, a promoter of this outrage? An oversize picture of this maritime hero hung above the dispatch window in the hall of the Sailors Union of the Pacific on First Avenue in Seattle, alongside a crude portrait of a union "martyr" in the 1934 maritime strike. This was Magnuson's explanation to the Senate on July 21, 1950: "Some of the last strongholds of Communism in this country exist in some of the waterfront unions. In my opinion the bill will have the dual effect of helping clean out whatever subversive influences may exist around waterfronts and of protecting the country from sneak attacks."[14]

To understand Magnuson's role in the Magnuson Act, consider waterfront union politics. At the time, maritime unions controlled virtually all jobs on U.S. flag vessels. The Marine Firemen, Sailors Union and the National Maritime Union supported the measure. Their reasons were mixed. There were genuine anti-Communists in these unions, seamen and longshoremen who knew firsthand that Communist Party members sometimes dealt from the bottom of the deck and worked from a hidden agenda. But alongside this ideology was infighting for union shore jobs—in seafaring parlance, "pie cards"—jobs as union agents, patrolmen, dispatchers. Under the Magnuson Act, a business agent wanna-be could remove a rival by snitching to the Coast Guard about the rival's association with a "subversive" organization.

Until the Court of Appeals ruling in 1955, the accused had no right to see the evidence against him or to confront the snitch. The Coast Guard quietly did all the dirty work in the name of national security.[15] Little wonder that Magnuson never boasted of his role in this outrage, not even during his 1950 race for reelection, when he was accused of being "soft on Communism." Perhaps he was ashamed. The Magnuson Act of 1950 was in tune with the times, but not with the senator's conscience.

Joe McCarthy never showed any shame. Off and running with his anti-Communist issue, reckless with his charges, absent a moral constraint about injury to others, McCarthy played the press like a toy drum. If one discounts his ability to ignore facts, this appears to have been his greatest talent. He understood a fundamental truth about reporters: they always sought "play"—more precisely, display with bylines—on the pages of their newspapers. They quickly discovered that Joe was virtually a cinch for play.

It worked like this: in the morning, McCarthy would call a press conference to announce that the names of "Comsymps" or "fellow travelers" would be given to the press in the afternoon. The afternoon papers would publish news of the announcement, and the morning papers would print the names themselves the following day. Next time he would reverse the process, announcing in the afternoon that names would come the next morning. He was playing "fair" with newsmen. Reporters went along with the game, and McCarthy got two cycles of news play for a single announcement of names.[16]

The game prompted Maurice Rosenblatt to comment, "McCarthy was a creature almost entirely of whole cloth, woven on the looms of typewriters. He ran a press circus with himself as ringmaster. His rise can be attributed to a press which covered him with fulsome fascination, as no senator has ever been covered before or since." Rosenblatt recalled scenes in the corridors of the Russell Building (née Senate Office Building), Joe emerging from a "closed" hearing, walking in front of a "gaggle of eager reporters, all looking for his words on what had happened in the hearing room. McCarthy would oblige, never mind how outrageous or unsubstantiated. For these walking, imitation news conferences, substantiation would come tomorrow—but tomorrow never came, and he got away with it."

There is no excusing this sorry episode in American journalism. It did grave damage to the reputations and careers of scores of so-called witnesses, who were in fact being accused either directly or by innuendo and who had scant means of redress or rebuttal. Hadn't McCarthy instructed them not to talk to the press after the closed hearings, and didn't this carry the implicit threat of a contempt-of-Congress citation? The reporters' rationale came from the steady pressure exerted by editors, especially wire service editors with twenty-four-hour news cycles, to "freshen the overnight leads"—the nightly rewrite of morning stories for editions to come the following afternoon. Joe knew this and usually accommodated.

Reporters' typewriters, however, were futile without play back home in their newspapers. No problem. McCarthy had unlimited support from the Hearst chain, with its eighteen newspapers coast to coast, from the wire service International News Service, and from the Midwest powerhouse—even bigger than Hearst in that part of the country—the *Chicago Tribune.* Along with hundreds of other papers, they lapped up Joe's charges, displaying them almost always on the front page. Commies, suspected or accused, were hot copy.

There were critics in newsprint, too: the *New York Times,* the *New York Post* (pre-Murdoch), the *New York Herald Tribune,* the *Washington Post,* the *Baltimore Sun,* the *Portland Oregonian,* the *St. Louis Post Dispatch,* the *Madison (Wisconsin) Capitol Times*—eight of the nation's best newspapers. All made McCarthy's select "left-wing list" for following a "pro-Commie" (that is, anti-McCarthy) line.[17]

But Joe's crusade was cruising past these critics, and Pat Hurley's vengeance was upon the State Department. Bowing to McCarthy's ominous pressure, the department fired ninety-one allegedly homosexual employees in 1952, thus reflecting the notion of Senator Kenneth Wherry of Nebraska that "you can't separate homosexuals from subversives—a man with low morality is a menace to government."[18] McCarthy had already denounced "Communists and queers who have sold 400 million Asiatic people into atheistic slavery . . . [through] powder-puff diplomacy."[19]

Nothing reveals so much about McCarthy's solipsism—his absence of gut convictions other than belief in what was good for Joe on any given day—as his relations with reporters. He liked them and frequently sought them out for drinks; he puzzled about why some of them didn't like him and disapproved of what he was doing. Didn't they know it was just politics? Just a ticket for reelection?[20] But he was getting from them and their employers a political career and, worse, a place in American history.

Sometimes Joe dipped into apparent self-pity over his self-appointed role as political savior: "It's a dirty, disagreeable job I have to do. I don't enjoy doing it, but the job has to be done."[21] Was he ambivalent or simply protesting too much for a man who seemed to enjoy inflicting pain?

In his "dirty, disagreeable job," Joe had no greater accomplice than William Randolph Hearst, a newspaper genius, no Johnny-come-lately to anti-Communism, and no friend of Democrats. In 1934 Hearst, a political Jekyll and Hyde, planted reporters under-cover to sniff out Communist faculty members at the University of Syracuse, the University of Chicago, and Columbia University. Decades earlier, William Randolph Jekyll had been a crusading populist, scourge of the beef trust, the oil trust, the railroad trust. As a friendly critic had put it, "Wherever you find foes of Hearst you find enemies of the people." He aimed to "raise hell and sell newspapers" and had no time for Pulitzer Prizes.[22]

But by the mid-1930s, W. R. Hyde had come to hate taxes, the New Deal—the "Raw Deal," the chief ordered his far-flung editors to call it—and above all Communists, or anyone so suspected. He told his readership, "Whether anybody else makes the fight against Communism and mob rule or not, I'm going to make it."[23] And so he did. By 1950, with Hearst's newspapers and one wire service behind it, anti-Communism—more specifically, McCarthyism—had, as they say in show business, legs.

Richard Berlin, first among several equals at the top of the Hearst empire, took charge after Hearst's death in 1951. Berlin did not diminish the anti-Communist crusade he had inherited. On the contrary. With his columnist George Sokolsky, or "Sok," Berlin played maker to the political marriage of Joe McCarthy and Roy Cohn, a federal prosecutor and the right-wing Sok's protégé. Cohn curried the favor of Sokolsky and his Hearst stablemate, Walter Winchell, through courthouse leaks to the columnists.[24]

Sokolsky's background, too, reads like a Jekyll and Hyde story. Early on a Trotskyite—a follower of the Soviet outcast and "enemy of the people" Leon Trotsky—he later became a hired propagandist for the anti-union National Association of Manufacturers and the Iron and Steel Institute. Some said he worked as a flack for imperial Japan. Five days before Japan's sneak raid on Pearl Harbor, in a masterstroke of bad timing, or worse, disinformation, Sokolsky claimed that the Japanese wanted peace.[25]

Sokolsky and Berlin consummated the McCarthy-Cohn connection in a meeting with the senator at the Astor Hotel in Manhattan. They insisted that McCarthy make Cohn his chief counsel on the Senate Subcommittee on Investigations—a problem for the committee chairman. Joe Kennedy, a major McCarthy financial backer, wanted his boy Bobby to have the job.

Maurice Rosenblatt related a scene in which Joe Kennedy drove up in a snowstorm to a Capitol Hill townhouse in the shadow of the U.S. Supreme Court building, where McCarthy and a friendly lobbyist were cooking steaks. Kennedy, wearing a homburg to thwart the snow, left the car's motor running. He met McCarthy at the door with an imperative: "I've got no time.

Bobby won't give me any peace. You've got to give him a job." Joe dodged, saying he'd take it up with the ranking subcommittee Democrat, John McClellan.

With his wherewithal and political clout, Kennedy usually got what he wanted. Not this time, or at least not exactly. McCarthy went with Berlin and Sokolsky: Cohn became his counsel. Bobby Kennedy settled for a job as counsel to the committee's Democratic minority and remained Cohn's enemy for life.[26]

To seal the deal, McCarthy named J. B. Matthews as his committee staff director. According to an unsigned memo leaked from the committee, Matthews's address was 363 Hearst Building, New York City, and his salary was paid by J. A. Clements, a Hearst public relations executive. Joe used Matthews's penthouse during his visits to Manhattan. There, among others, he met Alfred Kohlberg, Mr. China Lobby.[27]

Reinforced with Matthews, McCarthy's Senate Permanent Subcommittee on Investigations kept to the attack, frequently operating behind closed doors and striking at targets less vulnerable than China specialists. While some of his fellow senators pondered what to do about a colleague they considered out of control, McCarthy was bulling his way to a showdown with his nemesis, Maurice Rosenblatt, and the National Committee for an Effective Congress.

5 | The Hunter

"I WASN'T LOOKING FOR A TARGET—the target found me."
That is Maurice Rosenblatt's suggestion that his confrontation
with Joe McCarthy had the kiss, or maybe the curse, of the
inevitable, a fate rooted in the protagonists' history. Indeed,
Rosenblatt had a unique, premature political education, one
that carried through the McCarthy era.

"I had the advantage of gifted parents, a European immer-
sion, an accelerated childhood, and audacious self-confidence.
That was my patrimony," said Rosenblatt. "My parents were chil-
dren of the Enlightenment, mother a musician. We never owned
a car, but we always had a grand piano. The leitmotiv as we were
growing up was Chopin's preludes."

Frank Rosenblatt, Maurice's father, a native of Kiev with a
Columbia University Ph.D. in political economy, wrote a land-
mark study of the nineteenth-century British Chartists, work-
ing-class reformers of Parliament. Decades later, upon meeting
Maurice, the academic-turned-senator Paul Douglas exclaimed
to him, "Your father wrote a very important book!"

In the 1920s Maurice lived with his family in Vienna, where
his father was director of a privately funded effort to relieve
post–World War I hunger. His father traveled the continent,
once in Russia meeting with Leon Trotsky, a founding Communist revolutionary who, as he told his son, "would just as soon
shoot you as look at you."

At the dinner table in Vienna, Maurice heard continual
political discussions. On the streets outside he witnessed a continent in travail. Hunger, teamed with inflation, brought private
misery, political extremes, and violence.

The family did not suffer. On the contrary—the Rosenblatts lived in Viennese style in the Grand Hotel, where Maurice was schooled by private teachers, rigid disciplinarians paid $1 per day, a splendid sum given economic conditions. But outside Maurice saw panhandlers begging for a meal, workers trying to organize unions as Viennese cops tried to beat in their skulls. "Brot, nicht blut!" (bread not blood) was the chant of workers' demonstrations. As Maurice recalled it, "I was witnessing the decomposition of Central Europe." Across the German border, Adolf Hitler, a fast-rising tyrant, blamed all the trouble on Jews. Soon, so would his American imitators. Rosenblatt carried this premature education, this preconditioning, for the rest of his career.

Back home in a New York suburb, economically depressed like the rest of the nation, Rosenblatt had a brief interlude of his mother's cooking and free board before moving west to the University of Wisconsin. It was cheap—tuition $100 a year—liberal, and excellent. It was also in an uproar. If not as riotous as the streets of Vienna, the Midwest campus was a microcosm of the left-right polarity afflicting the economically distressed nation elsewhere.

This was 1932. Breadlines were growing, Wall Street brokers were peddling apples and, some said, leaping out of tall buildings. Franklin D. Roosevelt was elected president. A few months later Adolf Hitler, wild-eyed, mesmerizing, creature of Vienna's slum hostels, survivor of bedbugs and drunkards, was sworn into office as chancellor of Germany.

Rosenblatt did odd jobs for room and board, sat at the feet of academic icons—Alexander Mickeljohn, the philosopher, and Selig Perlman, the economist—and worked on the student newspaper, the *Cardinal.* He covered a ruckus between members of UW's mighty Badger football team and a rally of the League for Independent Democracy—a right-left encounter. Sans pads and helmets, the Badgers tossed two professors into Lake Mendota.

This was hot news on campus. The jocks had gotten their inspiration, Rosenblatt discovered, along with pocket money, from Badger alums in downtown Madison who wanted UW cleansed of "Commies." What better cleansing than the waters of Lake Mendota? It was Vienna redux, the powerful bullying their lessers. But it was the aftermath to this campus episode that shaped the hunter.

"Liberals on the faculty stayed quiet," Rosenblatt recalled. "The president, Glenn Frank, virtually went into hiding. The call for discipline came from a medieval historian and political conservative, university dean George Clark Sellery. He denounced both the football bullies and the downtown alums who would 'break down the University of Wisconsin.'" Rosenblatt wrote it up in a front-page story for the *Cardinal.* "In the clutch, it was a conservative who stood up, a conservative who had the courage," he remembered.

"It was my moment of maturity, my blooding, a profound lesson," Rosenblatt recalled. And later, when the student had a painful—Is there any other kind?—breakup with a coed, the dean sent him a note: "What care I how fair she be, if she be not fair to me." The young man carried the model of Dean Sellery, along with credentials as an editor of the *Cardinal* and the *Wisconsin Dairymen's News,* from Madison to Manhattan, where, like young people of generations before and since, he sought employment and glory as a journalist.

"What I saw on the streets of New York was what I had seen ten years earlier on the streets of Vienna," said Rosenblatt, who got a job on the *Advance,* a trade union sheet edited by the remarkable J. B. Hardman. It wasn't glory, but it was $25 a week. A job of any kind at that time and place was hard to find.

The violent confrontations he saw in Manhattan made campus conflict between "fascists" and "progressives" in Madison look like kid stuff. Rosenblatt wasn't the only acute observer. As James Wechsler reported in *The Nation* magazine on July 22, 1939:

> For six months New York has been somewhat incredulous watching the evolution of an anti-Semitic movement; its manifestations are angry and violent, it uses the streets as a battleground and it

employs all the familiar devices of an ancient crusade. Its spiritual leader is Charles Coughlin and its book of revelation is his magazine, *Social Justice.* . . . several stabbings, a multitude of street fights, deepening tensions in neighborhoods where clashes have become commonplace . . . they have been almost uniformly ignored by the press, partly because it fears to tread on Catholic toes, partly because it still believes in the silent treatment for anti-Semitism.

The Coughlin to whom Wechsler referred was Father Charles Coughlin, a radio speaker with an audience of millions and leader of the Christian Front, a group of street thugs, mostly Irish and thoroughly anti-Semitic. In Maurice's description, Coughlin was "a showman, huckster, and crowd-pleaser." Allied with him in anti-Semitism was Fritz Kuhn, boss of the German-American Bund, who got propaganda and inspiration from Josef Goebbels and, eventually, jail time for theft. Another player in the anti-Semitic movement in New York was Joe McWilliams, who led something called the Christian Mobilizers and who rode through the Manhattan streets in a horse-drawn wagon, holding a lantern in a vulgar replay of Diogenes, searching for an "honest Jew" and lashing out at "God's frozen people."[1] McWilliams drew crowds but never made the papers.

"Anti-Semites—Coughlin, McWilliams—were taking over the city," said Rosenblatt. "With the press blackout, politicians could ignore the danger." Maurice couldn't. This was the high water mark of American political extremism.

Rosenblatt took his frustration with the news blackout to the offices of Arthur Hays Sulzberger, publisher of the *New York Times,* and George Backer, publisher of the *Post,* and then to James Warburg, international banker and advisor to FDR. He was smart. He already knew how to open doors in ivory towers. He pushed the need for press coverage—and got nowhere. The publishers and Warburg were unmoved. They didn't want to publicize hoodlums or, fearing an anti-Semitic backlash against the newspapers, get their hands dirty brawling with thugs.

Still frustrated, Maurice turned from the boardrooms to the streets, recruiting students, some of whom he had known in

Wisconsin, from Columbia Law School, and the Union Theological Seminary. Soliciting for muscle, he called on John Santo, behind-the-scenes boss of the Transport Workers Union and, it would soon be revealed, the Communist Party organizer in the Bronx. Santo said no and warned, "It's very dangerous, what you are doing."

"Communists repelled me," said Rosenblatt—"too ideological, too dogmatic. They could be witty, as in this CP ditty of the time: 'An economic Tory had an awful scare; he went to sleep on Wall Street and woke up broke on Union Square.'" Although he didn't like Communists, at the moment anti-Semites repelled him more. He took his meager force to the Bronx, 139th Street and Third Avenue, where the dozen or so recruits passed out ecumenical literature and called for peace in the streets. They wore coats and preppy ties for an expected confrontation with 350 proto-fascists, the Christian Front backed up by Kuhn's Bundists. Cops and medics awaited the conflict.

"My heart almost stopped at the sight," said Rosenblatt. "Should I call off the showdown? No. We've come this far. We're not going to back down."

"It's the Kikes. It's the Jews!"—shouts from the mob as it struck. Blood trickled before the cops moved, but no injuries were serious and no arrests made. Next day Rosenblatt found a headline inside the *Daily News:* "Coughlinites Riot; Attack Divinity Students." Bingo! Right-wing Christian thugs attack unarmed demonstrators preaching peace in the streets.

"That headline was priceless," said Rosenblatt sixty years later. It was a breakthrough, the flip side of appeasement. It resonated—an awakening for the city's liberals.

The upshot: formation of the New York City Coordinating Committee for Democratic Action, directed by Rosenblatt and backed by Mary Lasker, wife of the public relations tycoon, and the Protestant Church Council. The committee, through a network of agents, gathered information on right-wing, pro-Nazi activity and published it in its magazine, the *City Reporter.* Rosenblatt's agents included Stuart McClure, a would-be writer, and Jane Gordon, ward of Bernard Baruch. Jane recruited her boyfriend, David McKeekan, a brilliant actor later to light up Broadway and Hollywood as David Wayne. Good scouts all. They were paid $25 a week.[2]

There was ample material for the *City Reporter,* especially concerning efforts by the anti-FDR German embassy to influence the 1940 election. The embassy had an ace on Capitol Hill, poet-propagandist George Sylvester Vierick, who wrote "FDR Is a War Monger, a Man on Horseback" and "Roosevelt Will Plough Under Every American Boy," referring to the New Deal policy of burying crops and slaughtering hogs to inflate farm prices, as well as "Now with unfolding eyes we see the paradox of every fight; that both are wrong and both are right; that friend is foe and foe is friend—and nothing matters at the end." German Foreign Office documents described Vierick as "the most valuable liaison agent."[3]

The committee kept an eye on Abwehr—German intelligence—agents, as well as Charles Lindbergh and the isolationist America First Committee, in which Lindbergh was a prominent figure. Rosenblatt was suspicious of activities going on around 10 Battery Street, headquarters for shipping firms and almost certainly under the watch of Abwehr agents. He passed on his suspicions to the NYPD's Alien Squad, whose members were eager readers of the *City Reporter.* Apparently they helped keep watch on suspected Nazis.

It ended with Pearl Harbor. Rosenblatt closed the committee's doors at 512 Fifth Avenue and joined the army, eventually tracking petty miscreants as a sergeant with the Criminal Investigation Division in New Guinea. As usual, the army found a place in a round hole for a square peg—in this case an expert on Nazi espionage chasing GI moonshiners.

Manhattan postscript: Not so coincidentally, Rosenblatt's New York City was becoming flooded with German Jews, lucky ones who did not doubt the meaning of Adolf Hitler's highly touted theory of a "master race," his code for a population without Jews. Some came to safety through the derring-do of Arno Viehoever, a mechanical engineer turned candle manufacturer in Santa Cruz, California. A written account of Viehoever's exploits, taken from a speech he made to the Santa Cruz Rotary Club in 1988, came to Rosenblatt through their mutual good friend, the lobbyist Joan McKinney.[4] This was the essence of it:

Viehoever, a near miss for a slot as a U.S. Olympic pole vaulter in the 1936 games in Berlin, went to Germany anyway, on money supplied by his rich Uncle Joseph. Arno's job was to finance the escape of thirty-two Jewish employees of Uncle Joseph's leather goods factory in Offenbach.

Hanging around the bar of the Hotel Vierjahrzeiten (Four Seasons), Munich's five-star hotel, favored by Brits and Americans, the playboy cum money launderer met the lovely, inscrutable Unity Mitford, daughter of an aristocratic English family, already famed in those social circles for taking her pet rat to a fancy dress ball.

Arno and Unity went horseback riding together a couple of times. But no romance—the lady was already enthralled by Adolf Hitler, her political hero, whom she had met over kraut, bratwurst, and beer at the Ostera Bavaria, a restaurant favored by the Nazi gang. The dictator already had a live-in, Eva Braun, but he must have felt that the daughter of an English peer was worth stringing along.

Accordingly, Hitler offered, and Unity accepted, several invitations to call at the Berghof, the boss's home in the Alps above Berchtesgarten, along with her Great Dane, Rebel. Arno was her escort on one of these occasions, driving his snappy Horch convertible up the mountain, past platoons of armed guards, as guests at Hitler's forty-seventh birthday party. The gang was all there—von Ribbentrop, Goering, Goebbels, and the birthday boy himself.

As Arno described it, "a fire roared in the Berghof's great fireplace. When Rebel saw Hitler standing in the middle of the massive living room, he ran up, knocking him to the floor, tail wagging, tongue licking. For me, that was the end of a myth: 'If a dog likes him, he can't be all bad.' Nonsense."

The gathering was nonpolitical, said Arno, talk casual— "Where did you learn German? What will you do when you return home? The symphonic music was beautiful. Here I was with the most ruthless man in the world, and what power did I have to do anything about it? Going back to Munich, Unity mentioned she had a revolver in the glove compartment. She looked to see if it was still there. It was, and I thought how close I was to changing history."

Arno's bloated money orders did not escape police attention. He was escorted to police headquarters to explain what he was doing with all that money. He responded, "'I spent it. I'm big spender. I drink a lot. I go to the opera.' I was scared. They said, 'You couldn't spend this much money.' I took a chance and said, 'Gee, the Fuhrer didn't say anything about this when I had lunch with him a couple of weeks ago.' I guess they thought, 'What in hell have we got here!' So they let me go. I was still scared."

Mission accomplished, workers safe in the United States, Arno went home. Unity, in conflict over war between England and love for Hitler, attempted suicide in Munich's English Gardens with her revolver. Brain-damaged but not dead, she lived until 1948.

6 Postwar and Palestine

MAURICE ROSENBLATT STILL HAD New Guinea mud on his
boots when he got back to Manhattan from the South Pacific in
1945 looking for work. What to do? "Wall Street held no lure,
neither did business—I wanted to be a journalist," said Rosenblatt, who hooked up with old friends. Among them was Rose
Kean, a Broadway star from Missouri and a pal of the playwright
Ben Hecht's.

The ambition didn't pan out—a few pieces for *The Nation*,
but nothing steady at any of the city's daily newspapers. Something more important loomed. Rose introduced Maurice to
Peter Bergson (née Hillel Kook), who had come to the United
States from Palestine in 1940, initially to save European Jews
from death camps and later to save those who had survived.

"Charming, witty, and seductive—women fell all over him,"
was Rosenblatt's impression of Bergson, whose postwar cause
was a homeland for the one hundred thousand Jews scattered
in displaced-persons camps around the European continent.
Bergson's charm worked. Rosenblatt was brought into the cause
with Bergson's promise of "an opportunity to make history." The
same thing worked on Hecht, another key recruit to Bergson's
born-in-the-USA organizations, the American League for Free
Palestine and the Hebrew Committee of National Liberation.[1]

Almost lost to history, save in the memories of surviving par-
ticipants, was the divisive, smoldering conflict between Bergson's
organizations and the established Zionist groups. Each had the
same goal—a homeland for displaced Jews—but they differed
over the shape and structure of that Promised Land. Bergson
aimed for a secular—not a Jewish—state, and he questioned the
right of Zionists outside Palestine to make decisions about the
nation-to-be. The two sides would be openly hostile.

"Bergson and his aide, Harry Selden, impressed me," said Rosenblatt. "They didn't talk much about German brutalities. Instead, they talked about the atrocities of indifference—the inaction. Their bitterest scorn fell on the official blindness on the part of the U.S.-backed British and the traditional Jewish organizations." Those organizations regarded Bergson's groups as "terrorists"—with some accuracy, given their backing of the Irgun, the Jewish army in Palestine engaged in a de facto war with Britain. Bergson, in turn, regarded them as "terrified," Rosenblatt said.

Maurice chose sides in the schism when he joined Bergson, his chief aide, Harry Selden, actresses Rose Kean and Ruth Chatterton, and a mix of Capitol congressmen and judges at the "Hebrew Embassy," a sprawling mansion at 2315 Massachusetts Avenue in Washington. In time Rosenblatt would use its fifth floor to pitch his cause to Senators Warren Magnuson, Dennis Chavez, and Wayne Morse—all of whom would have a hand in the creation of the State of Israel. He had a salary and a title—director of Washington operations for the American League for Free Palestine. In plain words, he was the league's Washington lobbyist. He explained that his cause was "to get the Jews out of the ghetto and the ghetto out of the Jews." He would argue for Israel, but—taking a page from Peter Bergson—against Zionists.

Rosenblatt quickly gathered momentum, organizing a committee of one hundred members of Congress who favored recognition of a new Israeli state. He had a magnificent recruiting tool in the ornate, elegant "Hebrew Embassy." Describing Bergson and his headquarters, Rosenblatt said, "Peter had style and a sense of its importance in winning friends and spreading influence." The mansion, built by the Marquis of Reading, one-time British viceroy to India, became party central for the homeland cause. Note that it was the "Hebrew," not the "Jewish," embassy.

"The difference between 'Hebrew' and 'Jew' is the difference between a nationality and a religion," Bergson wrote in a twenty-three-page letter to Chaim Weizmann, president of the

Zionist Jewish Agency, in April 1945.[2] By calling for a "Jewish Commonwealth," Bergson argued, Weizmann was aiming for a theocratic state. If he got it, what would be the status of Palestine's Muslims and Christians? "I propose we abandon the undemocratic idea," wrote Bergson. "We want a free state, not a Jewish state, just as there is no state religion in the U.S. . . . the Zionist position is disastrous for us Hebrews."

That letter put knives on the table. Rabbi Stephen Wise, head of the American Jewish Conference, wrote to Secretary of the Interior Harold Ickes, a supporter of the American League for Free Palestine, describing Bergson's organization as "irresponsible—existing to get money and names of non-Jews like yours."[3] The *Washington Post* described Bergson as a "nuisance diplomat," in contrast to Zionists, who represented "reputable Jewish organizations." Bergson said, "Rabbi Wise won't tolerate any other Jewish organization working for Palestine. He's stealing publicity and honor for himself."[4]

Back in Manhattan, it had been showtime for Palestine. While Rosenblatt was still soldiering in New Guinea, Hecht and Bergson had planted full-page ads in the *Times* and the *Post*, airing the plight of European Jews. More spectacular and bestirring, Hecht produced a pair of enormously successful and frankly propagandistic performances on the same subject. The pageant *We Will Never Die*, with words by Hecht and haunting music by Kurt Weill, opened in Madison Square Garden in March 1943, and the play *A Flag Is Born*, with its scathing criticism of Anglo-American Jews, premiered in September 1946.[5]

New York critics, in chorus, panned the plays as featuring "speeches that are too long, writing that is too purple" (*PM*) and "dubious poetry, political oversimplification" (*New Yorker*).[6] But the playwrights and the plotters got what they wanted: according to Harry Selden, money.[7] Even Mickey Cohen, a Los Angeles mobster better known for murder than for charity, dispatched an enormous "batch of cash." *We Will Never Die* raised more than $1 million while expressing Hecht's disdain for established Jewish organizations. *A Flag Is Born*, starring Paul Muni and a newcomer, twenty-two-year-old Marlon Brando, both working for minimum union scale, raised even more money and concern in New York and on the road in Chicago.[8]

Brando, at curtain time of a brilliant acting career, closed the play with a bitter soliloquy: "Where were you, Jews, when the killing was going on? When the six million were burned and buried alive in lime . . . where was your voice? There was no voice, you Jews of America. Nowhere! A curse on your silence." Later he explained: "I was outraged, along with most people, that the British were stopping ships carrying half-starved survivors of Hitler's death camps to a new life." (The British, between a rock and a hard place—Palestine's Jews and Arabs—wanted to ease conflict in their post–World War I mandate by halting Jewish immigration.) "The play," he said, "made me a zealous advocate for Israel."[9]

"I liked Brando," said Rosenblatt. "He had no sense of money, although given his talent, he could earn all the money he wanted. He was rather odd." *We Will Never Die* may have been forgettable, but Brando's creation of a washed-up prize fighter turned longshoreman ("I cudda been a contender") in *On the Waterfront* and the loutish Stanley Kowalski ("Stel-lah!") in *A Streetcar Named Desire* will endure as long as we favor film and stage.

From theater receipts, the league purchased a Navy submarine chaser and helped fund the Jewish underground—some say terrorist—army in Palestine, the Irgun. And more advertisements calling for a homeland for refugees. The ads played fast and loose with the names of congressional sponsors. In a stinging letter to Bergson in May 1943, Senator Harry Truman ordered his name withdrawn from the "Committee for a Jewish Army." He also noted Bergson's unauthorized use of Senator Ed Johnson's name. "This doesn't mean my sympathy is not with the downtrodden Jews of Europe," wrote Truman, soon to succeed FDR as U.S. president and the critical figure in the creation of Israel. "But you have abused your privilege."[10]

By 1947 the British wanted out. Palestine was a drain on the United Kingdom's depleted treasury, and Jewish-Arab conflicts were a drain on its soldiers' blood. A partition between Arab and Jewish sections by the United Nations was inevitable.

It came in 1947. Could the new State of Israel survive without U.S. recognition?

One of Rosenblatt's first targets in Washington, Warren Magnuson, frequently shared a whiskey with his old Senate buddy, Harry Truman. Magnuson's companion of that time, Ruth Overton, was the daughter of Louisiana Senator John Overton. With the beautiful Rose Kean on his arm, Rosenblatt made his initial contact with Magnuson at a party hosted by Ruth in the senator's apartment. Maurice knew where to hit the proper buttons.

Magnuson was already sympathetic. At the request of friends in Seattle, he had broached the issue of U.S. recognition of Israel with President Truman in the White House. He would go again. Out front, Magnuson put his name on an article for *Answer*, the house organ of the Hebrew Committee of National Liberation, calling for the resettlement of 1.5 million Holocaust survivors. "Before victory [in World War II] can be enjoyed, the future of Palestine must be settled," said Magnuson, sounding much like his new friend Rosenblatt.[11]

As the United Nations headed to a vote on what to do with Palestine, the Truman administration split. The White House, facing elections in 1948, leaned toward recognition of the potential new state; the State Department, under the estimable George Marshall, strongly opposed it. Marshall got so angry that he told Truman he would vote against his reelection if he opted for recognition. The CIA had warned that partition of Palestine and creation of a Jewish state wouldn't work.[12]

So had the American League for a Free Palestine. "We will never accept a partition of Palestine, but we will not use force [the Irgun] against it," Bergson wrote to the United Nations six months before the fateful vote in November 1947. The United States and the Soviet Union voted with the majority for partition, thirty-three to thirteen, and so Israel was created.[13]

There is no indication that Truman or even Magnuson was aware of the schism between Zionist and League aims. As Truman told State Department Mideast diplomats, "I'm sorry gentlemen, but I have to answer to hundreds of thousands who are anxious for the success of Zionism. I do not have to answer to hundreds of thousands of Arabs among my constituents."[14] Conspicuously absent in his exchange with the diplomats was any acknowledgment of Bergson's opposition to partition or his call for a secular Hebrew nation in Palestine. In May 1948, Truman formally recognized Israel, the new Middle East state.

Mission finished, if not accomplished, Rosenblatt closed the doors of the American League for Free Palestine. The dream of an ecumenical Palestine—"the only civilized and rational way to go," according to Maurice—closed with it. Decades later, in July 2003 at his home in Washington, D.C., I asked him whether the dream might have prevailed: "There's no yes or no answer," he said. "But I do feel partition between Arab and Jewish sections was bound to fail. Perhaps if a pluralistic, democratic state could have been imposed on Palestine within a generation, it would have worked."

Half a century after the founding of the new state, Peter Bergson, a founding father, gave a somber summing up. From his home in Shmaryahu, Israel, he wrote to Rosenblatt:

"I presume Israel is still of interest to you—although it may not match my obsession. After years of forced inaction I'm now going to launch a new [educational] campaign. Israelis must get rid of their inferiority complex and realize they are one of the most important nations in the world . . . an important manufacturing nation . . . a potential conduit between the Western republics and the emerging nations. . . . but it still depends very heavily on the United States.

"It is still in a permanent state of war with a hundred million Arabs. It maintains an army which is larger, I believe, than the armies of England, Germany or France. Yet as we approach our 50th year of war we still don't have a foreign policy geared towards peaceful existence. Instead, Israel accepts a destiny of perpetual war.

"We won spectacularly in 1967, and again in 1973. The problem with these great victories is that we aren't winning the war; we are only winning battles. Generals win battles. Statesmen win wars. We have no statesmen."[15]

*The good soldier Rosenblatt (standing, far right) and his military intelligence unit,
South Pacific, 1943. Major assignment: eliminate Army moonshiners.*

Roman holiday: Maurice Rosenblatt and Laura Barrone

*David McKeekan (aka David Wayne), actor and undercover agent for the
New York City Coordinating Committee, inscribed his photograph: "For Maurice,
who almost got me killed trying to save the Jews!"*

*Lobbyist and McCarthy
nemesis Maurice Rosenblatt*

*Maurice Rosenblatt, normally a man of
action, caught in repose*

Political allies and old pals: Eugene McCarthy and Maurice Rosenblatt

In a preview of Joe McCarthy, State Representative Al Canwell swears in a witness before his legislative committee investigating alleged Communists on the University of Washington faculty. Seattle Post-Intelligencer Collection, Museum of History and Industry

Democrats on the "McCarthy Committee": (left to right) Henry Jackson, Minority Counsel Robert Kennedy, John McClellan, and Joe McCarthy.
University of Washington Libraries, Special Collections, UW23623

The Carroll Arms Hotel, back stage to the Joe McCarthy drama.
"Exclusive and expensive," said Manager Jack Kloss. "After all, we cater to members
of the Senate, the world's most exclusive club."
Courtesy Library of Congress

En banc: The Permanent Subcommittee on Investigations. (left to right):
Senators Phil Potter, Everett Dirksen, Karl Mundt, Joe McCarthy (chair),
John McClellan, Henry Jackson, and Stuart Symington.
University of Washington Libraries, Special Collections, UW23624

Mission to Nanking: Secretary of State George Marshall (third from left); to Marshall's right is W. Walton Butterworth, U.S. minister to the Chinese nationalist government, and Chiang Kai-shek. Marshall's attempt to reconcile Chinese Communists and Nationalists failed, and civil war ensued.

Representatives Harold Velde, chair (seated, left), and Morgan Moulder of the House UnAmerican Activities Committee take a break during a hearing in Seattle.
Seattle Post-Intelligencer Collection, Museum of History and Industry

Witness Eugene Dennett knits while his attorney Ken MacDonald (right) studies the next move as they appear before the House UnAmerican Activities Committee in Seattle.
Seattle Post-Intelligencer Collection, Museum of History and Industry

Bergson sent this letter on August 27, 1993. He died a few years later. The war continues.

From Rosenblatt, though, no regrets. "For three years I'd worked for the creation of Israel," he said. "While the pay was only subsistence, the reward came in political capital, sufficient to launch my own lobbyist venture, sufficient for creation of the National Committee for an Effective Congress."[16] And sufficient for the most daunting challenge of any Washington lobbyist's career, the humbling of mighty Joe McCarthy.

Palestine Postscript: Although Maurice never mentioned it, Bergson's Hebrew Committee and Rosenblatt's American League for a Free Palestine were targets of intense FBI surveillance, 1943-47, through wire taps and a pair of snitches inside the organizations identified only as "T-1" and "T-2." The reports were obtained by the David S. Wyman Institute for Holocaust Studies. Apparently, they were instigated by the State Department at the request of the British Foreign Office, which had a "strong suspicion" that Peter Bergson was tied in with Palestinian terrorists—the Irgun.[17]

T-1 produced a detailed internal memo on talks with Senators Morse, Kefauver, Cooper, Gillette, and Jackson; the latter, according to T-1, "a very solid left Democrat." More revealing is the U.S. Communist Party hostility toward the Hebrew Committee ("irresponsible . . . harmful to the rescue of the Jewish people") and Rosenblatt's American League ("Jewish revisionists, fascist-minded agents of imperialism, sponsors of the Irgun terrorist group"). In contrast were the "solid Jewish organizations" and established Zionist groups, such as the American Zionist Emergency Council.[18]

7 | The Cause

WHEN PRESSED TO THE WALL of his comfortable home near the national Capitol, Maurice Rosenblatt was ambivalent, if not contradictory, about his history of political causes—the last, the most conspicuous and dangerous, the cause of exposing Joe McCarthy, a destroyer. Joe didn't tolerate enemies. He terminated them. Coming at the subject long after McCarthy's political destruction and death, Rosenblatt said, "I've never had a predilection for 'causes,' and I cringe whenever I'm assaulted by hard-breathing liberals, who, as Arthur Schlesinger Sr. said, 'are led around on a leash by an underdog.'"[1]

He continued: "When I was in the army, dealing with rookies, I said, 'The idea is not to die for your country but to make the enemy die for his.'" He sounded a lot like the cynical but steadfast prisoner of war played by William Holden in the movie Stalag 17, who is more interested in saving himself than the rest of the world. But the image doesn't quite fit Rosenblatt.

Along with his brief for nonscheduled airlines, Rosenblatt carried around the Capitol the lessons of J. D. Hardman, editor of the *Advance*, Dean George Sellery, the conservative academic who had risen (while liberals sat in silence) to smite the campus bullies in Wisconsin, and Peter Bergson, "the man of action, a man of purpose." He said, "Bergson and Sellery essentially taught me this: 'You've got a role to play—something bigger than yourself. You've got to take bigger steps.' With McCarthy I realized I needed to respond to his threat.

"It didn't come down like a bolt of lightning, but in steps. I realized I had a leadership function, that I could rally others and motivate them. I couldn't defer to others, I couldn't be a Polonius moralizing instead of acting. And I didn't see myself as just another adroit Capitol Hill operator. I had the kind of anger I felt confronting the Christian Front in New York. I wasn't going to yield.

"There were elements of defiance, bravado, adventure, and, yes, adrenaline. I was audacious. Hardman told me, men of purpose will take the gamble. You have to take a chance. Otherwise you won't know for sure you can make it. If you know in advance you can make it, the effort is no fun.

"I didn't see McCarthy as a personal challenge. It was bigger than that, much broader. In a small way, I wanted to make history."

In his twelve-volume *A Study of History*, Arnold Toynbee wrote of civilizations advancing or crumbling, given their response to challenges. Too much challenge and they are overwhelmed and collapse, but with sufficient response to the challenge, they survive and thrive.[2] Where Polonius sat back, talking, Rosenblatt responded, gambling. He didn't go under. Accordingly, he would thrive—and by his notion have fun.

By the new year, 1953, the gamble of his career was under way. Joe had to go—no bolt of lightning, just an accumulation of observations leading to the judgment. "McCarthy was a mean guy—a villain in the democratic process," said Maurice. One especially distasteful event was McCarthy's sneering, bullying, personal attack on the Senate historian, Richard Baker, whom he scorned as a "left-wing Democrat." "It was strictly against Senate decorum to hit on a staff man," said Rosenblatt. "It showed a man so swollen with power he could ignore such institutional disciplines. I didn't like it."

From the Capitol corridors and cloakrooms, Maurice's allies in the Senate, among them Dennis Chavez of New Mexico, began crossing the street to the Carroll Arms for quiet meetings. Senator Lister Hill, an Alabama populist and a favorite of FDR's—"Lister Blister," the president called him—came early one morning at the start of the new year, dispatched by Lyndon Johnson, the Senate majority leader. Washington had not softened Hill's Southern drawl; Rosenblatt said he talked like Stepin Fetchit, the Hollywood comedian who played the stereotypical

Negro servant. But he was ahead of his time as a progressive, helping to legislate education and health-care reforms. Widely respected, Hill also served as Johnson's tie to Southern conservatives.

"'Maw-reese,'" Rosenblatt remembered Hill saying, "'we've got to get that guy [McCarthy] while he's still on the rise. The Leader [Lyndon Johnson] says you've got to get a Republican point man. Democrats will follow.' Then he pushed his knuckle into my chest and repeated, 'You've got to get that rogue!'"

As they talked, Cohn and Schine came downstairs from their top-floor suite, smiling.

On another day, still early in January, Robert Kennedy showed up at the Carroll Arms. It was his first day on the job as a member of Joe McCarthy's investigation staff. Rosenblatt recalled a confrontation: "I was by the newsstand when Kennedy approached me, eyes blazing, hurling a string of curse words at me. 'What's got into you?' I asked. He said, 'You sonofabitch. You know what I'm talking about. Those stories!' I had written a piece for *The Reporter* magazine on his father, Joe Kennedy.

"He continued to curse me. I was speechless. There was a pause. Then he grabbed me and tossed me onto a couch in the lobby. His eyes were still blazing as he went off to meet McCarthy and the senator's entourage. As his father once said, Bobby is a great hater. I subsequently ran into him two or three times at parties. Each time he cut me dead, looking the other way. Bobby Kennedy for president? No!"

The new year, 1953, had begun with bang.

It was a critical time in the anti-McCarthy operation. But had Rosenblatt, Hill, Chavez, and "the Leader" known what McCarthy was doing behind the closed doors of his Subcommittee on Investigations that year, the matter would have taken on even greater urgency. The full story of those hearings lay buried for half a century until, in 2003, the transcripts of the proceedings were released by the Senate.

8   The Closed Hearings: Vengeance and the VOA

ON FEBRUARY 13, 1953, the *Chicago Tribune*, by its own admission the "World's Greatest Newspaper," bannered across page one, "Uncover Plot in 'Voice' to Sabotage U.S." The byline gave the name Willard Edwards.

"Voice" was Voice of America (VOA), the radio propaganda arm of the United States Information Agency. The time was one of a peak in Americans' concern over Communist infiltration of their government and, not so coincidentally, in the power of Senator Joseph McCarthy, the new chairman of the Senate Permanent Subcommittee on Investigations.

Ruth Watt, the committee's chief clerk, later told Rosenblatt she had informed McCarthy that Senator John McClellan, the outgoing chairman, planned to leave the committee. Quick to respond, McCarthy called the Arkansas Democrat, according to Watt, and said, "You've got to stay on the committee to keep that sonofabitch Joe McCarthy in line." He was capable of humor.[1]

It was not that Americans had no real concerns. Ethel and Julius Rosenberg had recently been convicted in federal court of transmitting to the Soviet Union secrets of the United States' successful effort to make an atomic bomb. They would be executed in an electric chair at the end of that spring. Reds running America's radio propaganda as well as stealing its most guarded atomic secrets? "Comrats" losing China to Communists? So it seemed to many Americans.

Beneath that street-sales grabber of a headline, the Tribune's Edwards wrote: "A Senate investigation of Communist influence in the Voice of America uncovered amazing evidence of a conspiracy to subvert American policy in the nation's radio propaganda broadcasts." And further: "Scores of witnesses have involved high officials in a detailed account which indicates deliberate sabotage of American objectives in foreign propaganda. . . . closed door questioning developed a picture of such appalling proportions [that] executive sessions were ordered. . . . strictest secrecy concerning testimony was ordered by Roy Cohn, chief counsel."[2]

Ruth Watt told Maurice that "witness protection" was McCarthy's reason for closing the doors, "because he was still looking out for people. . . . if there was nothing there, he [the witness] was excused and nothing more was said." The reality was something else.

"Strictest secrecy" at these closed hearings was a joke. Stronger than before the 1952 elections, McCarthy allowed friends, sweethearts, and selected, friendly reporters, such as Edwards, to attend. No television. That would come later, but at the end there was Cohn, Schine, or Joe himself outside the hearing room to greet and brief an eager, compliant press. As he explained, "I always give a resumé [of proceedings] to the press. Otherwise a leak could come from one member and they [the press] get a very distorted picture."[3]

Edwards's story was as phony as Cohn's claim of secrecy and McCarthy's concern about "distorted leaks." Based on innuendos or biased assertions from fewer than half a dozen—not a score of—dubious witnesses, it likely came from leaks by Cohn or McCarthy himself. It is hard to believe that a reporter present at the hearings could have mangled fact and testimony so badly—even one with a determined ideological slant, like Edwards.

We know of McCarthy's conduct of the "closed" sessions, and thus of the distortion of Edwards's report, from transcripts made public in January 2003, fifty years after the fact, by the Senate Committee on Government Operations. "Basically, McCarthy could do anything he wanted," said John Adams, counsel to the U.S. Army. "He gave quite a show, including the impromptu press conferences to say what had happened in the closed hearings."[4]

That was not overstated. After the three Democrats on the committee walked away from it over a personal dispute, McCarthy was questioned about the absence of a quorum. Joe, who was still there, replied, "There is a quorum present. Under rules of this committee one person constitutes a quorum"—so long as the chairman was present. And this, he said, had been approved by the Senate as a whole.

What McCarthy wanted, most of all, was evidence to back his round-the-news-cycle assertions of Communist subversion inside the U.S. government—plus a measure of revenge on his enemies. Never mind the means or due process. Nothing in the four volumes of committee transcripts—four thousand pages of small print—provides redemption for a senator long since deemed a bully, obsessed, unfair, and perhaps a tad off his rocker.

Nor does glory shine upon the Democratic members of his subcommittee, Senators Stuart Symington, John McClellan, and Henry Jackson. With rare exceptions, the transcripts show them as silent witnesses to ruthless interrogations by McCarthy, Cohn, and the committee's unpaid counsel, G. David Schine. They were probably intimidated.

Some five hundred witnesses—credit McCarthy with determination to find a Commie—came before this inquisition. There were two categories: friendly witnesses, convinced that there were subversives inside VOA, and not-so-friendly ones, fearful for their jobs but determined not to be bullied into something they deemed harmful to U.S. interests. The "friendlies" wanted VOA to broadcast hard-core, never-mind-the-subtleties, anti-Communist propaganda.

McCarthy's heart must have leaped with the testimony of Robert Bauer, of VOA's Latin American division. Joe asked Bauer why VOA beamed juvenile adventure programs south of the border, instead of bare-knuckled anti-Commie material. "Was it an honest mistake or a deliberate attempt to sabotage VOA?" asked Joe. In either case, McCarthy's assumption was clear: it was wrong. "I don't know," Bauer answered. "We had a hard-hitting program we wanted to put on . . . but one easy way to sabotage it would be to use [VOA] money for ineffective products. I don't know one person [in VOA's overseas service branch] I would call a good American. . . . I can't say they are

Communists, but—there is that smell."[5]

Another friendly, Nancy Landkeith, testified that the French desk ran "pro-Communist themes." These included a discussion of America's "Negro problem" and comments such as "America has no culture, is incapable of serious thought, unimaginative and materialistic." Besides, said Landkeith, the French desk was loaded with "atheists." She identified herself as a Catholic.

Roy Cohn fed her a pregnant line: "Do you think the scripts show disrespect and disapproval of the American way of life?"

"Yes, I did," Landkeith answered.

"What do you think of Marcelle Henry [a VOA script-writer]?" asked Cohn.

"I think she is subversive," said Landkeith.

"That VOA material [by Henry] would sound more like the voice of Moscow, I gather," said McCarthy.

"Exactly," snapped Landkeith.

"Any programs on religion?" asked Cohn.

"Christian programs alienate the French," she answered. "They are taken to be atheistic."[6]

Ah, the smell.

From the friendly to the suspect. The committee interrogated one Harold Vedeler of VOA's East Europe desk, accused of soft-peddling propaganda into Czechoslovakia.[7] Cohn: "Were you ever a member of a subversive organization?" A— "Not that I know of." Q— "Were you a regular reader of *PM? The Daily Compass?*"—both left-of-center newspapers now long defunct. A— "No." Cohn ordered Vedeler to make a list of all organizations to which he had belonged over the previous decade. Presumably, Vedeler complied rather than face a contempt citation.

Vedeler was small fry compared with a red-hot suspect, Reed Harris, deputy administrator of the International Information Administration, overboss of VOA. What made Harris so hot was his decision to suspend Hebrew language broadcasts to the Middle East. This came at a time when Jewish leaders in Soviet-controlled Czechoslovakia, notably Rudolf Slansky, were on trial for their lives and soon to be executed. McCarthy viewed this as obvious material for hard-hitting anti-Soviet stories broadcast in

Hebrew and aimed at Israel. He was ignorant that at the time, Hebrew, Israel's official language, wasn't the one most commonly used there. German, Yiddish, English, and French were more popular in that five-year-old nation of immigrants.

Nevertheless, on February 23 McCarthy suggested that the decision was "sabotage" and asked Harris, a smart, formidable witness, if he was a Communist. "No," said Harris, "I'm anti-Communist." He had cancelled the Hebrew broadcasts to save money.[8]

But Harris was vulnerable. In the description of an admirer, Maurice Rosenblatt, Harris had been "a college liberal at Columbia, perhaps naive." As such he had edited the campus newspaper, the *Spectator*, and in 1932 wrote a book critical of payoffs to Columbia football players, conditions in the college cafeteria (unclean but managed by the university president's sister), the politics of the American Legion, and the necessity of religious, as opposed to civil, marriages. The book, *King Football*, as Harris would come to acknowledge, was more sophomoric than serious.

Well, said Inspector McCarthy, if Reed Harris wasn't a Commie, then his critique of the American Legion and religious weddings followed "the Communist Party line. . . . If you had been a Communist at the time, this is the type of book you would have written."[9]

Joe surely sensed "the smell." He called witnesses who had known Harris: Nathaniel Weyl and Donald Henderson. Weyl said he "had the impression" in the mid-1930s that Harris was "pro-Communist, but I can't substantiate it."

Henderson, an economics professor at Columbia, took the Fifth Amendment when asked if Harris was a Communist. The chairman judged that this reply implied Harris was a Communist, for otherwise Henderson would have answered the question. Joe had a thing about the constitutional right to avoid self-incrimination: "An innocent man doesn't need the Fifth Amendment."[10]

Harris's book had caused the college president to drop Harris from Columbia. McCarthy told the hearing that Columbia had "expelled him for radicalism." No, said Harris, he was suspended from classes but later reinstated. Help came from a lawyer dispatched by the American Civil Liberties Union (ACLU). Twice in his interrogation McCarthy noted Harris's connection with the ACLU: "Do you know they have since been listed as a front for and doing the work of the Communist Party?" Harris said he didn't know this and how could he have?—the ACLU never having made the attorney general's lengthy list of alleged subversive organizations.

The harrying would go on for hours, by sneaky implication condemning the witness. McCarthy did it like this: "The hearing had been closed because the charges made here against you are of such damaging nature to you, if true, that we felt the committee should examine all aspects of the situation and hear you in executive session." He continued: "I am very, very, interested in getting to the bottom of why certain things happen and finding out who is responsible and if there is incompetence, stupidity, or deliberate sabotaging of VOA. . . . the book you wrote in 1932 is straight from the Communist Party line. Why were you selected for this job? It's almost like [Secretary of State] Dean Acheson selecting me to write his memoirs."[11] That was meant to be a joke. No pals, Joe and Dean.

Exasperated, Harris declared, "I have been an honest and loyal employee of this government from the first moments . . . [and now] you are dealing with something that affects my whole life, the life of my family." Finally, a sympathetic glimmer comes through in this relentless, gloomy inquisition. Senator Henry Jackson, noting Harris's statements of opposition to Communism, asked, kindly, whether he could produce any anti-Communist writings. "I think I could forgive your youthful indiscretions if you have something [in writing] to counteract the book [*King Football*] you wrote in 1932," said Jackson. Harris had nothing of the sort on hand, but in the context of the hearing, it was nice of Jackson to ask.[12]

McCarthy would later examine Harris in a televised hearing, some of it shown, with appropriate comment, in Edward R. Murrow's documentary "See It Now," a deconstruction of Senator McCarthy that aired on CBS on March 29, 1954. "Senator McCarthy succeeded in proving Reed Harris had once written a bad book, which the American people had proved by not buying it," summed up Murrow.

Deeply shaken by the ordeal and, by implication, accused of subversion, Harris resigned from VOA in April 1954, one month after the televised hearings. In a happy twist of fate, he returned to the propaganda agency in 1961, hired back by Ed Murrow, President Kennedy's choice to head the U.S. Information Agency. "Reed never really got over the shock of McCarthy's smear through interrogation," said his friend, former VOA counsel Richard Schmidt. "The hearings were awful for Reed, a decent, intelligent man." Harris died in 1981 of natural causes.[13]

Raymond Kaplan died on March 5, 1953, the last day of the Harris interrogation. He threw himself under a truck on a Boston street rather than face questioning by the Subcommittee on Investigations. The VOA engineer left a suicide note for his wife and son: "I have not done anything in my job which I did not think was in the best interest of the country, or of which I am ashamed. And the interest of my country is to fight Communism hard. I am much too upset to go into the details of the decision which led to the selection of the Washington [State] and North Carolina sites [for VOA transmitters]. . . . My deepest love to all."[14]

Another VOA engineer had claimed in testimony that the transmitter located at Port Angeles, at the top of Washington's Olympic Peninsula, was inferior for broadcasting U.S. propaganda to the Far East and the Soviet Union—a problem with magnetic storms. Better to have placed the transmitter in California. It looked to Joe like another Commie plot to sabotage VOA.

Yet another witness, Dorothy Fried, a secretary in the Washington VOA office, was asked by Roy Cohn, "Are you now or have you ever been a member of the Communist Party?" "No, sir," she answered. "Let me ask you this," McCarthy interrupted. "Do you know whether [Raymond] Kaplan was a member of any

Communist fronts or whether he belonged to the Communist Party?" "I know nothing about his personal life," she replied.[15]

Nor could any other witness connect Kaplan with Communism. But the committee allowed the question—the smear—to linger: Why else would Kaplan have killed himself except to avoid questions about placing a VOA transmitter at Port Angeles and thus undermining America's effort to instruct the Far East? Such insinuations wrecked careers and created headlines but produced no charges against any of VOA's managers or employees. If he had been fishing instead of Commie hunting, McCarthy could be said to have been skunked.

But he was undeterred, not embarrassed even at the testimony of Nancy Stalcup Markward, a snitch for the FBI inside the Communist Party from 1943 to 1945. She had served as "membership director" for the Washington, D.C., cell assigned to recruit new members, which, she cheerfully admitted, she did.[16] It amounted to a make-work project for federal investigators. Markward recruited Commies, and G-men busted them.

Vengeance, not the pursuit of treason, carried McCarthy into the interrogation of Russell Duke and Ed Morgan. This was in January 1953, and the target was Oregon's acerbic Senator Wayne Morse, a particularly troublesome critic of Senator McCarthy's.

Duke was a Portland influence peddler ("public relations executive") close to Morse, and Morgan, a Washington lawyer, was counsel for the subcommittee chaired by Millard Tydings that had found McCarthy's celebrated Wheeling speech "a fraud and a hoax."

McCarthy was unforgiving. He questioned Duke ("I was pretty big in Oregon") on an alleged fee-splitting arrangement with Morgan for settling an income tax claim of $100,000 against Dr. David Tang Lee. Duke supposedly got $8,000, and Morgan, $4,000, for getting Morse to address the Internal Revenue Service. Morse confirmed he had called the IRS on behalf of his constituent, Dr. Lee.

Some embarrassment followed: "My ethics are on trial for communication with this man [Duke]," said Morgan. But no charges. Morse brushed off the business as constituent service. Morgan had gone to Wisconsin to campaign against McCarthy in 1952, and Joe might have felt good about himself in the role of a "Mr. Clean" at work in the Augean stables of payoff politics in Washington, D.C.[17]

Theodore Kaghan, director of public affairs for the U.S. High Commissioner in occupied Germany, labeled Joe's amateur hit men, Cohn and Schine, "junketeering gumshoes" after they told the Berlin press that Kaghan had "strong inclinations to Communism." McCarthy called Kaghan before his committee for several hours of hostile questions.[18]

Kaghan, a newsman, author, and playwright in the early 1930s, had signed a petition to place a Communist on a local election ballot and had worked alongside Joe Barnes on the foreign desk of the *New York Herald Tribune*. McCarthy asserted that Barnes, who had helped General Eisenhower write his memoir, *Crusade in Europe*, was at least a suspected Commie. Worse, Kaghan had roomed with a known (but never named) Communist and had stated in one of his plays that "Communists are people, too." Besides, Roy Cohn didn't take at all kindly to that crack about junketeering gumshoes.

Inspector McCarthy noted all of this and wondered how—wink, glower, nod—if Kaghan had worked with Barnes at the *Herald Tribune*, he could then have come to be pushing an anti-Communist line on behalf of Americans in Germany. But it didn't click. McCarthy got no further than this insinuation against Kaghan, who had a letter from the Austrian chancellor praising his "courageous anti-Communism," as well as security clearances from professional U.S. gumshoes. He apparently kept his job.

Even McCarthy's contempt citations were shaky.[19] Harvey O'Connor, a Seattle radical, ex-logger turned editor of the socialist *Seattle Daily Call*, took the Fifth Amendment when asked if he was a Communist. Outside the hearing room he answered the question: "No," he said, he never had been. Joe cited him for contempt of Congress. He was convicted, given a one-year suspended sentence, and fined $500—a judgment soon reversed by an appeals court. "I got caught in a brawl between McCarthy and the State Department," explained O'Connor, whose books on the Astors and the Guggenheims, nineteenth-century capitalists, were found by Cohn and Schine on the shelves of American libraries in Germany. Schine supplemented McCarthy in questioning O'Connor.

The chairman got even less revenge in his futile effort to settle a score with General Telford Taylor, the chief prosecutor at the Nuremberg war crimes trials after World War II. In a speech to cadets at West Point in December 1953, on May 16, 1954, Taylor had labeled McCarthy "a dangerous adventurer" making "groundless and shameful charges in an unscrupulous grab for publicity." He gave a reprise of that speech to Jewish war veterans in New York on May 6, 1954, noting the "fear and hysteria" aroused in the nation.[20]

Maurice Rosenblatt had first known Taylor in Manhattan. They became reacquainted in Washington, where Maurice found a suitable house for Telford and his wife, Mary, on Connecticut Avenue. "Telford was a New Deal lawyer, a card-carrying liberal, very crisp," said Rosenblatt. "You didn't mess with Taylor, and he couldn't suffer fools. I think he considered McCarthy a card-carrying sonofabitch."

Taylor's New York speech was a reprise of one he had made earlier at West Point. Within a week of his West Point attack on McCarthy, on December 8, 1953, Philip Young, chairman of the Civil Service Commission, was called before McCarthy's committee for questioning about Taylor's confidential personnel file. Someone—never identified—had flagged the report with the note, "unresolved question of loyalty." And someone breached its confidentiality by leaking the file to the investigations committee. McCarthy bore down hard on Young:

Q: Is Taylor loyal?

A: That flag means that if he applies again for a federal job, his file should be rechecked.

Q: But the flag means he is disloyal.

A: The flag itself doesn't mean he is disloyal. It's merely a warning to check his record.

McCarthy managed to squeeze a minor concession from the witness, summarizing by saying, "The flag means there was an investigation showing derogatory material and it was never resolved whether he was disloyal or not."

"A correct statement, sir," said Young.

"That is all," said McCarthy, dismissing the witness.

And that was it, save for the inevitable leaks of innuendo and suggestions of "disloyalty." No call came for Taylor to testify, nor was any investigation made of the alleged "derogatory material."[21] "If Telford had not been so self-controlled, I think he might have physically assaulted McCarthy," said Rosenblatt. "Fortunately, he was smart enough and disciplined enough not to do that."

"McCarthy was judge, jury, prosecutor, and press agent in these hearings," said Erwin Griswold, then dean of the Harvard Law School.[22] Looking back on McCarthy today brings to mind Franz Kafka's Inspector.

9 | The Inspector and His Witnesses

IF NOT NICER, the image of Senator Joseph McCarthy coming out of the fifty-year-old transcripts of his "closed" committee hearings is at least more complex than that of the one-dimensional inquisitor who appeared in the televised hearings in early 1954, the so-called Army-McCarthy hearings. Those later hearings left most Americans with the image of a scowling, bullying abuser of citizens' rights, though some saw a rugged savior of freedom from Communism. TV tended to bring out the darker side of the man.

In the transcripts, several Joes can be seen. There is, of course, Joe the bully, forsaking, in his phrase, the "lace handkerchief" for the gnarled fist in his search for Commie rats inside the recesses of government. There is also Joe the comforter, a kindly sort who really doesn't want to kill your career and ruin your reputation: just the names of Commies, please, which might include you, the witness. Finally, the transcripts, released forty-five years after McCarthy's death from alcoholism, give a rare glimpse of Joe the stymied, a bully getting as much as he gives.

Hanging over the witnesses called before these hearings—and there were hundreds of them—was the threat of a contempt-of-Congress citation and sometimes a threat of perjury charges. Nothing in the techniques "the Inspector" used on these witnesses would come as a shock to anyone in a metropolitan cop shop, where the business is to get a confession, never mind a little verbal dishonesty. It beats bamboo sticks under the fingernails.[1]

In his probe of suspected "subversion and espionage" inside the research facility of the Army Signal Corps, on October 16,

1953, McCarthy called Jack Okun, a radar technician. Roy Cohn asked Okun whether he had roomed with another Signal Corps researcher, one Harvey Sachs. Okun said that for a "few months" he had.

Cohn: "Did you know Sachs was a Communist?"

Okun: "No, sir."

McCarthy: "He [Sachs] never admitted he was a Communist?"

Okun: "No."

McCarthy: "Your testimony is contrary to [that of] other witnesses. . . . Either they perjured themselves or you have been." The matter would be turned over to the Justice Department.

A fortnight later, on the same trail of Signal Corps subversion, McCarthy called Harvey Sachs before the committee and fired a battery of questions at him about his alleged Communist connections. Sachs had little to say. In an earlier interrogation McCarthy had told Sachs, "Go get a lawyer who is not a Communist—a good honest lawyer. Then return and come clean."[2]

"We won't spend any more time to get this information with pliers," McCarthy threatened. "We have testimony about you, a great deal of it. . . . you are not telling the truth, or someone else has perjured themselves."

McCarthy noted that Sachs had roomed with Jack Okun, who was "Communistically inclined." He ordered the witness to prepare a list of all of his roommates, as well as places stayed and the date he started work at the Signal Corps.

Missing in this record is testimony from "other witnesses" alleging that either Sachs or Okun was a subversive. Joe was bluffing, an old cop shop trick. Nor does the record show any charges having been filed against these witnesses for either perjury or contempt. Sachs and Okun might even have kept their jobs.

Chief among the Inspector's weapons was the bluff. As he told Benjamin Wolman at the Signal Corps hearing, "We know something about you. You can go commit perjury if you care to. I do not care." Wolman refused to answer the question of whether his wife was a Communist, but when Joe asked whether she had been a Communist before their marriage, Wolman answered no.

"He has committed perjury," said McCarthy.[3] The record does not indicate that Wolman was so charged.

"You have been identified under oath as a member of the Communist Party and an important functionary in *Amerasia*, a tool for Soviet espionage." So McCarthy opened an interrogation of Harriet L. Moore Gelfen. She had written a book for the U.S. military on Communism. "You are a very, very important functionary of the Communist Party."

It was a tough shot, based, for a change, on actual testimony. That testimony had come from Louis Budenz, by then a professional anti-Communist tattletale with a less than sterling record for tattling the truth. But the record does not indicate that Gelfen broke and turned songbird. This time it was a busted bluff.[4]

Almost sweet is the transcript of the interrogation of Allen Lovenstein, of the Signal Corps laboratory, by committee staffer Robert Jones. "I don't know if you know this," said Jones, "but nothing you say here will go outside this room. . . . it's just [an opportunity] to unload your heart, more or less, and will help us immensely in proceeding."[5] That sweet-talk amounted to a lie. McCarthy and Cohn were prolific in their "off-the-record" leaks of committee interrogations to eager newsmen waiting to lap it up outside the hearing-room doors, apparently unconcerned that they were taking in a slanted version.

One hapless witness admitted, under questioning, that yes, he was a subscriber to *The Reporter* magazine. It's gone, now, still lamented, and not to be confused with the New York City Coordinating Committee's *City Reporter* of the 1930s. While it lasted, *The Reporter* was a liberal, vigorously anti-Communist journal, edited, published, and financed by Max Ascoli. Joe told the witness that the magazine, "as far as we know is the successor to *Amerasia*, a strictly Communist party-line paper. The editor is Mr. Ascoli. He is a Russian who takes it on himself to try and crucify anyone who hurts the Communist party line."[6] *The Reporter* was also anti-McCarthy.

Max Ascoli, born in Ferrara, Italy, in 1898, was a lawyer at odds with Benito Mussolini's Fascist regime. A Jew, he came to the U.S. in 1931 on a Rockefeller fellowship, taught political science, married an heiress, and, in 1949, with her wherewithal, financed *The Reporter*. It paid top dollar for top journalists, including Albert Ravenholt and Joe Miller.[7] Maurice Rosenblatt, an acquaintance of Ascoli's, remembered him as "very Italian, volatile, given to explosions of temper and giving people nasty names." His magazine's demise, ironically, was attributed partly to its hostility toward the radical left in the 1960s. Joe's inability to distinguish an Italian from a Russian immigrant must be attributed to political bias. Sadly, the record shows no attempt by anyone on the committee or its staff to correct McCarthy's errors of fact or to challenge his judgment.

McCarthy comes across as downright soothing in his questions to Carter Lemuel Burkes, a reluctant witness. "This is not a threat," he says. "This is just friendly advice I'm giving you. Do you understand that?" And later he asks Burkes whether he has always preferred "our system of government to the Communist system." When Burkes answers yes, McCarthy immediately replies, "You understand, of course, it is no crime to prefer Communism to our system. You have a right to prefer it. I am not saying you do [prefer Communism], you understand."[8]

The tale told by Victor Rabinowitz, a leftist lawyer whose clients had appeared before McCarthy, is almost poignant. Rabinowitz approached McCarthy in a Senate hallway to make a plea on behalf of Sylvia Berke, a clerk at Public School 50 in New York City's Bronx: "He [McCarthy] stepped out of a Senate elevator, saw me, and with his usual geniality, which he exhibited only in personal relations, he threw his arms around me, shouting, 'Hello, Vic. What can I do for you?'

"We went to a private room adjacent to the elevator. I asked whether he would excuse Sylvia from testifying . . . that it seemed unnecessarily cruel to this young woman to deprive her of employment in a situation that made it possible for her to work and raise a child, albeit on a very low salary.

"She is going to take the Fifth Amendment anyhow, so the committee would get no information from her. McCarthy's answer: 'It's all right with me, but you'd better take it up with

Roy.' Cohn was standing nearby . . . his answer was quick and peremptory: 'Nonsense, we can't withdraw the subpoena.' I told him since she was going to take the Fifth Amendment the only result would be that she would lose her job. It made not the slightest impression on Cohn."⁹

So Sylvia Berke came before the committee on November 4, 1953, Rabinowitz at her side. She said no when asked if she was a member of the Communist Party. She took the Fifth Amendment when asked if she had been a member in the past.

"Did you drop out of the Communist Party so you could come here today—under instructions of Communist Party officials—and say you were not a member?" asked Cohn.

"No," she answered.

Cohn was determined not to take no for answer. "Who instructed you to drop out of the Communist Party?" he asked.

"I'm not saying anybody did," Berke replied. "I'm not saying I ever was a member."

McCarthy seemed exasperated at the woman's dance, from her answers about the present to her use of the Fifth Amendment when questioned about her past. He raised the flag of patriotism in an apparent reference to the war in Korea, where U.S. troops were engaged against a Chinese Communist army: "In view of the fact that the Communist half and our half is at war, and a great number of our young men have died in the shooting part, do you think any good American should keep from the proper government officials his or her knowledge of the members of the Communist conspiracy?

"I cite the Fifth Amendment on that," said Berke.

"I'd like to see some of these Fifth Amendment cases in Russia and see them cite the Fifth Amendment," concluded McCarthy, hustling Berke offstage. ¹⁰

The chairman's attitude toward potential witnesses before his committee is best revealed in his warning during an investigation of the Army Signal Corps facility at Fort Monmouth, New Jersey: "Even though you think the man [witness] is completely innocent, keep this in mind, that the most dangerous agent is the man who looks like a Sunday school teacher."¹¹

In neither looks nor manner would Paul Hacko have suggested a Sunday school teacher. An employee of General Electric, a veteran of World War II, Company E, 105th Infantry, and a sometime candidate of the socialist American Labor Party for Congress, Hacko had been around. His itinerary, he testified with reluctance, included a stint inside the Communist Party as an FBI snitch. He gave back as much smack talk as he got from the Inspector. Besides, he was grouchy, having responded to a committee subpoena delivered only the night before. McCarthy frequently applied the quickie summons, presumably to catch the witness unprepared and thus more easily intimidated.

It didn't work this time. After McCarthy's now familiar overture to an interrogation—"Are you now or have you ever been, etc."—Hacko interrupted: "You are not going to put words into my mouth. I say this committee is illegal."[12]

Joe: "Don't talk while I'm talking."

Hacko: "Proceed."

Joe: "I'm going to ask you about Communist Party connections and about espionage."

Hacko: "I object. You are stating that I am a Communist and I object."

Joe: "Look, mister, you are going to act like a gentleman."

Hacko: "I am a gentleman and I believe you are not a gentleman."

Joe: "Will you be quiet?"

Hacko: "I will leave."

Joe: "Marshal, stop this witness."

Hacko: "You are taking away my Thanksgiving turkey."

Joe: "Do you want additional time?"

Hacko: "I don't want anything from you. Maybe Mister Schine does."

Joe: "We have testimony you are a Communist."

Hacko: "That's a lie. . . . You make me sick. You are doing more harm to the U.S. government than anyone else."

Joe: "Can you get over being sick long enough to answer questions?"

Hacko: "I haven't even had breakfast. I don't think I can.

You can hold me in contempt. . . . I'm walking out of here."

Joe: "You are not. . . . Are you an espionage agent of the Communist Party as of today? . . . Has the Communist Party ordered you to obtain information about work at GE [General Electric]?"

Hacko: "Who said I belonged to the Communist Party? What do you mean 'ordered'? . . . Why don't you stop that line? . . . I am under your orders. All you need is a swastika and a helmet and you will be right in your place."[13]

Joe: "Look, mister. We have a very important job to do here and it is not pleasant to sit here and listen to people like you rant and rave."

Hacko finally answered no, he was not an espionage agent, or a Communist, and left. McCarthy must have been relieved. It's easy to imagine that Paul Hacko might have left the witness table to cheers and congratulations had the hearing been open to the public.

Hacko would not be asked to appear in subsequent televised hearings.

Nor would Benjamin Zuckerman, another reluctant witness. McCarthy, exasperated, made a hypothetical question from Zuckerman's testimony: "If I told you what you just said, wouldn't you think that either I was the damndest liar you ever heard or that I was a case for a mental institution?"[14]

Zuckerman let the pregnant question hang.

10 | The Clearinghouse

POWER MAY CORRUPT ITS USER. Even a little bit may loosen the constraints of morality or judgment. But it may also blind. The user can't see the point at which he goes over the line, at the wrong time with the wrong subject, to become—against his self-interest—an abuser. Joe McCarthy, "the most influential demagogue" in American history,[1] began to have problems with his political vision. Inside the Senate club, Joe got reckless.

His charge of disloyalty against Owen Lattimore, an obscure scholar and State Department advisor with an unfortunate facial twitch, might bestir negative emotions from a not-yet-prominent Washington lobbyist like Maurice Rosenblatt. But—and McCarthy knew this by intellect and instinct—it played well with a large number, possibly a majority, of everyday Americans, who were already suspicious of "eggheads" and not yet suspicious of the Wisconsin senator.

The "club" was something else. Early in 1952, from the Senate floor and thus safe from a legal charge of slander, he accused an aide to Senator Carl Hayden of having given a security clearance to an economist who was the subject of no fewer than "twelve separate FBI reports." The accused aide had worked for the State Department's loyalty board.[2]

Hayden didn't like it. He demanded that McCarthy prove his charge. McCarthy blew the demand aside, dismissing Hayden as an "old, blind fuddy-duddy."[3] McCarthy made an enemy. Hayden did have eyesight trouble, but which of the antagonists was the more blind? Another carelessly created enemy was Harry Byrd of Virginia, chairman of the Senate Finance Committee and, like Hayden, a conservative Democrat.

But McCarthy's fall was far from certain in 1952, much less imminent, despite liberal outrage against him in the Senate. William Fulbright (whom Joe called "Halfbright"),[4] Herbert Lehman, Mike Monroney, and Guy Gillette, as well as Carl Hayden, made anti-McCarthy speeches. Another, and the most conspicuous, was by William Benton, who said, "McCarthy is a hit-and-run propagandist of the Kremlin model."[5] They all complained of McCarthy's "un-Senate-like behavior—his breech of the club propriety."[6] These critiques fell as harmlessly as butterflies against a brick wall. For a time they may even have worked to McCarthy's advantage outside the Washington beltway. For a spell, the words "courageous" and "McCarthy" came together for a vast number of Americans caught up in anti-Communist emotions: here's a straight-shooting guy standing up to those Commie-coddlers, who can't take his kind of Americanism.

When Guy Gillette invited Joe to appear before the Subcommittee on Privileges and Elections to reply to Benton's charges of impropriety, McCarthy was insulting: "Frankly, Guy, I have not and do not intend to read, much less answer, Benton's smear attack. I'm sure you realize the Benton-type material can be found in the *Daily Worker* [Communist Party newspaper] any day of the week and will continue to flow from the mouths and pens of camp followers as long as I continue my fight against Communists in government."[7]

The futility of efforts by Joe's liberal critics was obvious. "I saw a tremendous vacuum," recalled Rosenblatt. "Men with good intentions, like Bill Benton and Herbert Lehman, standing out in a no-man's-land, attacking McCarthy—and not making a dent. With my background of opposition to right-wing extremists, it was inevitable that the committee [National Committee for an Effective Congress] and I would become involved with Joe McCarthy."

To fill the vacuum, in the spring of 1953, while Joe waged his investigations behind (sort-of) closed doors, Rosenblatt formed the McCarthy Clearinghouse as a congressional watchdog arm of the NCEC. He analyzed the need for it and stated its aims in a fifteen-hundred-word confidential memo to Robert

Nathan, chairman of Americans for Democratic Action (ADA), on March 4, 1953:

"[We] must start operating on the [Capitol] hill . . . no question that this is the only way [to stop McCarthy] and that nobody is doing it or even thinking about operating in any concrete realistic fashion. . . . The strategy involves working with [congressional] Committees. . . .

"The McCarthy–[William] Jenner–McCarran group are going after the machinery of government. . . . McCarthy has already created the precedent of being able to control-by-inhibition the State Department and our foreign policy because he has blitzed the personnel. . . . McCarthy exists only in the vacuum liberals have created.

"Can't liberals use the simple [lobbying] techniques of a God-damned power company?"[8] The NCEC would raise the money; the Clearinghouse would do the legwork.

Organizational help came from Dean Francis Sayre, the Washington Episcopal bishop; Harry Selden, late of the American League for Free Palestine; and Stewart McClure, Maurice's New York aide turned administrative assistant to Alabama Senator Lister Hill, "Maw-reece's" partner in the anti-McCarthy operation. To keep a record of McCarthy's speeches, news clips, and assorted other data—material that became ammo for the McCarthy opposition—they hired a full-time researcher, Lucille Lang, and rented a one-room office in the Carroll Arms. Wherewithal came from well-heeled liberals, among them Marshall Field and Paul Hoffman, a pal of President Eisenhower's and president of Studebaker autos.[9] Money flowed through the NCEC.

"Our purpose was to contain and oppose McCarthyism at the source of its power—the Congress," said Rosenblatt in an interview. In a memo, unaddressed but apparently meant for Clearinghouse backers, the organizer noted, "A head-on assault can't really hurt McCarthy since this is not a logical contest but a struggle for power."

In June 1953, a breakthrough. Rosenblatt spied a one-paragraph story on a back page of the *Washington Post.* It said that McCarthy had appointed one J. B. Matthews as staff director of the investigations subcommittee. Bells rang. Maurice asked Lucille Lang, the $75-a-week Clearinghouse researcher, for a background check and, if it turned out as he expected, to spread the word to friendly reporters.[10] These included the *Post's* Murray Marder, Clark Mollenhoff of the Cowles newspaper chain, Phil Potter of the *Baltimore Sun*, and the columnist Jack Anderson.

Lang found what Rosenblatt suspected in an old copy of the *American Mercury* magazine, in a piece titled "Reds in the Churches," written by J. B. Matthews. In it Matthews said that "the largest single group of the Communist apparatus in the United States today is composed of the Protestant clergy." He specifically shook an accusing paragraph at G. Bromley Oxbam, bishop of Washington, D.C., and close friend of Senator Harry Byrd. Lang spread the word.

J. B. Matthews had a jigsawed political background. He was a native of Hopkinsville, Kentucky, where church and state were close enough to ignore the differences and where church came before play, the Holy Bible before the local newspaper. The only institutional rival to the church was the Hopkinsville Hoppers, the Class D baseball club of the oldest organized minor league, the Kitty League. Matthews, a Methodist with a pleasant smile and a paunch, became an ordained minister. He would move from the social Gospels of the New Testament to Marxist socialism and then reject that conversion to preach the new gospel of anti-Communism.

Matthews taught the early edition, the socialist one, at Fisk University in Nashville, a predominantly black college, and he wrote a book, *Partners in Plunder*, a denunciation of capitalism cum Christianity. It claimed that J. P. Morgan ran the Episcopalian Church and Andrew Mellon bossed the Presbyterian congregations. Then Matthews flipped sides.

The "new" Matthews called *Partners* a "nasty stinking book" and asked the Lord for forgiveness. Turning hard right, he became a rising star, feeding anti-Commie material to his favorite columnists, Fulton Lewis Jr. and Westbrook Pegler, both Hearstlings.

In February 1953, soon after Matthews's conversion, the Christian Front gave a dinner in his honor, with Hearst columnist George Sokolsky as master of ceremonies. The guests included a who's who of America's right-wing militants—Roy Cohn, Alfred Kohlberg, Merwin K. Hart. Sokolsky read a message from Vice President Richard Nixon, a "white-collar McCarthy" in Adlai Stevenson's description. The event marked Matthews's turn from a liberal "gospel" to a right-wing one.[11]

Even before he found McCarthy, Matthews found a pulpit before the House Un-American Activities Committee, where he declared Adolf Hitler's dictatorship nicer than Joseph Stalin's,[12] which is akin to saying the needle is nicer than the rope for executions. Maybe, as Stalin once said of a rival before he had him shot, Matthews had become dizzy with success. His charge that "at least 7,000 Protestant clergy in the United States are serving the Kremlin's conspiracy" wasn't very smart.[13]

News produced by the Clearinghouse about Matthews's attack on preachers "stirred up the biggest hornet's nest you ever saw," said Ruth Watt, chief clerk to the Subcommittee on Investigations, who otherwise described the ex-Communist turned preacher turned tattletale as an able administrator. The news was too much for Senators Henry Jackson, John McClellan, and Stuart Symington, the Democrats on the subcommittee. They demanded that McCarthy fire his new staffer. When he refused, the three resigned from the subcommittee in July 1953.

Months later, under some pressure from Eisenhower, McCarthy relented. He dumped Matthews and agreed to hire Robert Kennedy as counsel for the committee minority. Accordingly, the Democrats resumed participation.

It was a telling episode. For perhaps the first time, the man who had turned anti-Communism into a spectacular political career had suffered damage. As Rosenblatt noted, the Matthews affair "demonstrated McCarthy's vulnerability." Word began to filter through the Senate cloakroom.

One anti-McCarthy speech, based on data collected by the NCEC's Clearinghouse and delivered on the Senate floor, hit a nerve with both Democrats and Catholics. In it, Senator Dennis Chavez of New Mexico, a frustrated member of the Senate Democrats' Policy Committee, chaired by Lyndon Johnson, denounced Louis Budenz, an ex-Communist turned professional anti-Communist informer. Rosenblatt recalled that he helped Chavez draft the speech, but not its most memorable line: "This man [Budenz] is using the Catholic Church as a shield. My ancestors brought the cross to this country"—Chavez was a descendant of early Spanish colonists of New Mexico—"and this man is using it as a club."

What prompted this speech, Chavez told Rosenblatt, who related their conversation in an interview, was the unwillingness of Johnson and the policy committee to attack McCarthy. On the contrary, "they talked about stealing Joe's thunder by attacking the State Department and chasing homosexuals. They didn't want to go over McCarthy. They wanted to go under him." Chavez was disgusted.

Jim Farley, the Democratic Party chairman, called on behalf of New York's Cardinal Spellman to rebuke Chavez. The archbishop of Santa Fe demanded that he recant, a demand reflecting the Catholic Church's tolerance of McCarthy. Chavez answered that this was none of the church's business—it was a matter of politics, not faith and morals.

McCarthy kept charging. In early July 1953 he told the army's congressional liaison, General Miles Reber, that he wanted a direct army officer's commission for G. David Schine. His investigator was about to be drafted as a buck private. It was a few weeks later that his committee began investigating Army Signal Corps employees in New York and alleging that subversives were operating at Fort Monmouth, New Jersey. Having savaged American Far East experts, Voice of America, and U.S. libraries in Europe, McCarthy's rampage escalated from the State Department to the U.S. Army.

For thirty-five days in the late spring of 1954, the question "Who promoted Irving Peress?" would overshadow domestic and foreign affairs, including the loss of Dien Bien Phu by French colonials to a force of Vietnamese guerrillas. Who was Peress? He was an army major, a dentist, who was given automatic promotion to lieutenant colonel. A sometime civilian lefty, he might have been characterized by McCarthy as drilling from within. Actually, Peress was a pretext for tackling another established authority, the U.S. Army, which had refused, for obvious reasons, to give G. David Schine an automatic officer's commission.[14]

Ruth Watt, the veteran committee clerk, said the pressure on behalf of Schine came from his close buddy, Roy Cohn: "Well, Roy worked with Schine all the time and they went on trips—of course we couldn't pay his [Schine's] expenses, but he didn't have to worry about money—where he got a lot of it, I don't know . . . he wasn't on the payroll. Then he went into the army and Roy was the one who did all that stuff trying to get him out. Of course Joe McCarthy could have cared less, but he did it for Roy." (Mrs. Watt later described McCarthy as "a very kind man, very thoughtful of people working for him.")[15]

The Clearinghouse opposition still wondered what to do. In July 1953 Rosenblatt met with Paul Hoffman, Francis Sayre, Harry Selden, George Agree, Millard Tydings, Robert Nathan, William Benton's attorney Gerry Van Arkel, and Drew Pearson's attorney Warren Woods—the gifted hard core of McCarthy's enemies. "We all had agreed to challenge the demagogue," said Rosenblatt. "Obviously we were doing something wrong. We needed to reexamine our assumptions. Where should we turn? Nobody wanted to take that step [to a censure motion], to lead the fight. To tangle with McCarthy was a very, very scary thing. He was abusive. There was no exit. . . . most people had nothing to hide, but it was a contagious fear."[16]

Gerry Van Arkel helped crystallize the group's strategy. As revealed in a letter to Benton, he likened the tactics of "Taft conservatives"—a reference to the Senate allies of Robert Taft of Ohio—in 1953 to the nurturing of Adolf Hitler by German industrialist-conservatives in the 1920s and 1930s. The German conservatives thought Hitler would be useful to them, just as the "Taft group" thought they could use McCarthy. "Tragically mistaken," said Van Arkel of both groups. It was only a matter of time, in his view, before McCarthy turned on Eisenhower and his secretary of state, John Foster Dulles.[17]

Stewart McClure refined Van Arkel's analogy into the keystone of opposition tactics. "Why, hell," he burst out at a Clearinghouse meeting, "McCarthy isn't even anti-Communist." Instead of fighting Communists he was pursuing Americans—Lattimore a prime example—who didn't conform to his attitudes. He wasn't a conservative but a radical, an extremist in tactics and objectives bent on tearing down leaders and institutions of the republic.

"In Stewart's analysis," said Rosenblatt, "McCarthy was fighting the establishment. What we had to do was to pit him against those establishment pillars. We had a firm strategy." Their game plan: jujitsu.

The new Senate minority leader, Democrat Lyndon Johnson, kept an eye on the Clearinghouse opposition from the sidelines. As Rosenblatt analyzed it, "Democrats are milling around without leadership or purpose—but they might back [an anti-McCarthy] move by Republicans.[18]

Indeed, Johnson would rationalize McCarthy as "a Republican problem." He was acutely aware, however, that he and Joe shared common benefactors in Hugh Roy Cullen, Clint Murchison, and H. L. Hunt, Texas oil and gas tycoons of right-wing persuasion. Besides, he commented, "Joe will go the extra mile to destroy you."[19]

As a service to his petroleum patrons, Johnson had stooped as low as Joe to destroy the chairman of the Federal Power Commission, Leland Olds, a pro-consumer New Dealer regarded by the Texans as hostile. At confirmation hearings in 1949, Johnson cited Olds's early writings to insinuate that he had been a Communist sympathizer in the 1920s. The oil-and-gas boys dug up the dirt; Johnson used it well. Olds's confirmation was rejected, his spirit wrecked. But gas profits rose.[20] It was a textbook example of personal demolition, a lesson Joe might have taken.

For the balance of 1953, McCarthy kept moving toward his showdown with the U.S. Army, questioning the promotion of a suspected "Comsymp," Peress. Lucille Lang kept stashing McCarthy data in the Clearinghouse files. And public adoration of the make-believe tailgunner soared to poetry. Two samples, with my apologies to Sir Walter Scott:[21]

> *A Tear for the Beautiful* (author unnamed)
> Breathes there a man with soul so dead
> Or interest in affairs so slight
> Who never fervently has said,
> "How I admire McCarthy's fight."

> *McCarthyism Is Patriotism*
> Come one and all and hear me say
> About a knight this very day
> Whose armor bright is truth and play
> 'gainst foes who would this land betray.
> The lefties and the eggheads spout
> In press and radio
> To spread their potent lies about
> There are no depths they will not go.

In late December 1953, Rosenblatt and his companion, Laura Barone, took time out. Given entrée by Senator Chavez, they went to Rome to call on Pope Pius II, the former Cardinal Pacelli, a one-time emissary to the Church in Bavaria. Rosenblatt's aim was to flip the Catholic leadership away from its sponsorship of McCarthy. He and Laura also needed a vacation. Laura took an apartment in Rome's modern section, and Maurice pulled more wires to gain the meeting with Pius II.

His Holiness was well-traveled and sophisticated, and Rosenblatt figured he could talk straight with him on topic A—Joe McCarthy. He wanted to explain that McCarthy was a liability to the Church and get the message back to Cardinal Spellman in New York. Father Cosgrove, of the American College in the Vatican, opened the last door, and Maurice got his interview with the pope.

"Where are you from, my son? How are the [Brooklyn] Dodgers doing?" the baseball-savvy pontiff inquired when introduced to Maurice, who closed to the point. "Your Holiness has added status to McCarthy," he said. "McCarthy is exploiting your approval." The pope listened carefully, and years later Rosenblatt described him as "an eighty-nine-year-old chief executive with amazing energy. It's hard to measure the impact of our meeting, but at least, word got back to the U.S. that Joe didn't speak for the Vatican. Subsequently, U.S. bishops sent out a letter [stating] that Joe didn't speak for the pope."[22]

Laura and Maurice stayed on for six weeks, meeting Rome's American press at the bar in the Excelsior Hotel, hitting the night spots along the Via Veneto, where the American singer Bricktop starred, and purchasing paintings from Mario Russo, a popular Roman artist of the time. The press bought the drinks at the Excelsior and wanted Maurice to fill them in on His Holiness. Rosenblatt obliged: "He was dressed plainly, except for red slippers; slightly stooped but very alert and bright. The clatter of Olivetti typewriters fills the Vatican's inner chambers—a very busy place." Later he described the pope as "a shrewd and worldly politician, in certain ways resembling Lyndon Johnson." A key difference, said Maurice: "Pacelli's wit was sophisticated, Johnson's earthy."

Back in the United States, beneath the prose and poetry surrounding the mighty Joe, was the reality of the U.S. Senate, a house evenly divided between Republicans and Democrats in 1953, leaving Republican Vice President Richard Nixon decisive. The Senate was where McCarthy's fate would be settled, a fact most apparent to McCarthy and the Little Joes, or, as Rosenblatt labeled them, "the Snaggle-Tooth Gang"—Senators Herman Welker, Styles Bridges, and Mollie Malone. Harry Cain had lost his place in the Snaggle-Tooth lineup by losing his seat to Henry Jackson in 1952.

With the loss of Cain, a change of one member in the ornate chamber would have greatly comforted McCarthy and his backers. The gang got a break on June 9, 1953, when Lester C. Hunt Jr., son of the senator from Wyoming, was arrested in a Washington park and charged with soliciting a homosexual act from an undercover cop.[23] Senator Hunt, a popular conservative Democrat, was up for reelection in 1954. If he could be persuaded to step aside, to forgo a reelection race . . .

Hunt, Rosenblatt said, didn't like McCarthy, "a drunk, liar, and opportunist" in the description of the small-town dentist turned politician. Apart from those unattractive characteristics, McCarthy had come to the defense of German soldiers charged with killing 150 U.S. prisoners of war at Malmedy, Belgium, after the Battle of the Bulge in World War II. This happened during a Senate hearing on the massacre, and Joe, no doubt, was making a play for Wisconsin's German-American vote. Hunt didn't like it at all.[24]

Shortly after junior's arrest, Hunt got word, relayed from Senator Herman Welker, that his son would not be prosecuted for this misdemeanor—thus avoiding the newspapers in Washington, D.C., and Wyoming—if the senator did not seek reelection. Hunt's response: he refused to be blackmailed. Three weeks later, on July 3, the *Washington Times Herald* carried a story about young Hunt's homosexual solicitation. Subsequently, he was judged guilty and fined $100.

Having made the D.C. press, the story of Hunt Jr.'s disgrace would surely become a campaign issue in Wyoming. Senator Hunt was in deep conflict over his obligation to fellow Democrats and the adverse publicity his run for reelection would create.

On a Saturday morning in his Carroll Arms suite, Maurice Rosenblatt took a call from Mike Manatos, Hunt's administrative assistant. The man sounded so distressed that Maurice asked, "What's the matter?" The matter was the suicide of his boss, who could no longer handle the conflict. He had killed himself inside his Senate office with a .22-caliber rifle shot to the head.

Newspapers played the suicide on Hunt's admission of poor health. The columnists Drew Pearson and Marquis Childs came closer to the truth. They linked his death to the threat of blackmail by Welker and his ally, Styles Bridges. Welker, the Idaho senator, appeared bereft of outrage or propriety. He gave a eulogy on the Senate floor for the late Hunt. His brass brought this response from Hunt's cousin, William Spencer, of

Chicago: "I was shocked when I read this [Welker's eulogy]. I recall vividly my conversation with Senator Hunt a few weeks before he died, wherein he recited in great detail the diabolical plot you [Welker] played following the episode in which his son was involved.

"Hunt told me without reservation the details of the tactics you used to induce him to withdraw from the Senate. It seems apparent you took every advantage of the misery the poor fellow was suffering at the time in your endeavor to turn it to political advantage. I understood too, from Hunt, that Senator Bridges had been consulted by you and approved of your action."[25]

In the last analysis, McCarthyism appears not only to have savaged many political reputations but also to have corrupted several of its followers and even killed one of their Senate colleagues. It seems to have had a life of its own—indeed, one that endures in some Americans to this day, more than four decades after the senator's death. McCarthy is "a misunderstood American hero," says Ann Coulter, a television commentator and author of *Treason: Liberal Treachery from the Cold War to the War on Terrorism*.[26] Coulter's thesis is that McCarthy, by himself, "saved America from itself for thirty-plus years" and that "the myth of McCarthyism is the greatest Orwellian fraud of our times."[27] In her terminal judgment, "the primary victim of persecution in the McCarthy era was [Joe] McCarthy." Her solution to the contemporary riddle of anti-American terrorism: "We should invade those [Muslim] countries, kill their leaders and convert them to Christianity."[28]

McCarthy and his "ism" surely resonated.

11 | Flanders and the Fall

FOR ALL THE CALCULATION AND SKILL of the Clearinghouse opposition, the sound and fury of his determined liberal critics, and the enmity of powerful Democratic conservatives, Senator Joe McCarthy's ultimate Senate foe was an "outsider," a self-made Vermont businessman turned Republican senator, Ralph Flanders. He would also be the most visible foe, but working with him closely behind the scenes would be Maurice Rosenblatt and his Clearinghouse colleagues.

Unconcealed but so far unpublicized, the Rosenblatt opposition was busy. It had a network of Capitol Hill operatives—congressional aides, staffers, insiders with access to congressional offices—not formally organized but in agreement that "Joe must go."

"You can't use hacks or fanatics to work the Hill," said Rosenblatt of this ad hoc network. "They were practical people who knew their way around."[1] But they were insiders, not directly connected with the American political mainstream.

One of them working inside the belly of the beast was Gracie Johnson, a snitch employed by McCarthy's Senate investigations subcommittee. A good-looking woman with a heart of gold, she had been recruited through Rosenblatt's friend Chickie Chaiken, a member of Senator Gillette's staff—no love lost between Gillette and Joe. Gracie was a close friend of Senator John McClellan, a crusty Methodist from Arkansas and a member of McCarthy's subcommittee. She was somewhat girlish about their relationship: As she explained to Rosenblatt, "Everybody knows I have a guest room."

For a time she kept a room at the Carroll Arms, the transfer point for committee documents headed into Lucille Lang's

Clearinghouse data bank. Gracie provided inside dope on who was who and doing what in the McCarthy apparatus. This heightened the role of the Carroll Arms as backstage to the McCarthy theater playing on the Senate floor.

A detailed record of telephone calls from subcommittee headquarters in December 1950 exposed McCarthy's high-powered contacts. Gracie's purloined telephone log showed calls from committee investigator Don Surine to the gifted right-wing columnist Westbrook Pegler and to William Randolph Hearst Jr., eventual successor to his father as boss of the Hearst news empire. J. B. Matthews called his boss, W. R. Hearst Sr., from the office. Another Hearstling, George Sokolsky, used the telephone to talk with Archbishop Cushing in Boston. His compatriot Ralph DeToledano called Richard Nixon from committee offices. Thank you, Gracie.[2]

By early 1954, American hysteria over treason on behalf of Communism had a household name, "McCarthyism," and such potency that no seer could have foreseen the rush of events that within a year would destroy McCarthy as well as his hold on public opinion. He was heading into a fight with the U.S. Army and an unflattering spectacle on coast-to-coast television.

Signs, however, still indicated a demagogue on the rise.

In February, McCarthy's committee got a $214,000 appropriation to investigate what the senator called "very, very current espionage" at Army Signal Corps headquarters at Fort Monmouth, New Jersey. More telling, votes for this appropriation came from liberals Hubert Humphrey, Estes Kefauver, Warren Magnuson, John Kennedy, and Mike Mansfield. The only vote against more money to fund Joe McCarthy's stumbling investigations was that of William Fulbright. McCarthy was still frightening. Those liberals, minus Fulbright, felt vulnerable.[3]

Joe's prose turned rancid, as in this sample from a floor speech: "Men and women wear the [Democratic] party label, stitched with the idiocy of Truman, rotted by the deceit of [Dean] Acheson, corrupted by the Red slime of [Harry Dexter] White." White was a high official in the Treasury Department who may, in fact, have been a Communist.[4]

Riding high, maybe giddy from that fat appropriation, McCarthy went further, labeling Democrats "the party of betrayal," responsible for "twenty years of treason." A week later he declared General Ralph Zwicker, a soldier of proven bravery, "not fit to wear the uniform," for he had "coddled Communists" by promoting Major Irving Peress, the army dentist.[5]

That was a bit much for the mild-mannered army secretary, Robert T. B. Stevens. He denounced McCarthy's "humiliating treatment" of Zwicker. Not so, replied Joe. His treatment was "too temperate," and moreover, Stevens was "one of the finest dupes I ever met."[6] Presumably that was meant as a compliment.

Later, in his accustomed quick, "off-the-record" press conference, McCarthy gloated, "I made that little sonofabitch [Stevens] get down on his hands and knees and beg to me." On this day, however, a reporter balked. Phil Potter of the *Baltimore Sun* told Joe he would not observe "off the record" and would report his comment on Stevens. And so he did. It was a key factor, said Potter's friend Albert Ravenholt, in turning President Eisenhower against the senator.[7]

In the midst of these exchanges, Senator Flanders took the floor to caution that McCarthy was diverting attention from "dangerous problems abroad" and splitting the GOP at home. Problems abroad would have included the real or perceived threat of a Soviet invasion of Western Europe—the United States was hastening to re-arm Germany and transfer two new army divisions to reinforce NATO—and the war between French colonials and Vietnamese guerrillas in Southeast Asia.[8]

Flanders, a self-educated machinist who had worked his way up from machine shop apprentice to mechanical engineer, had already taken his measure of McCarthy and found him wanting. He might well have agreed with Albert Ravenholt's appraisal of the man: "a fake." McCarthy's defense of the 1944 German massacre of American prisoners did not go down well with the crusty Vermonter.

Joe was undaunted. Flanders carried little weight in the Senate club. And there was this business with the army. McCarthy wasn't getting anywhere with his demand that G. David Schine, soon to be drafted as a buck private, be given an officer's commission. Then, inexorably, it was showtime. In a bizarre twist in McCarthy's conflict with the army, open hearings before a Senate committee were carried live via television into virtually every American living room and tavern, starting on April 22, 1954.

For the next three months, in what were called the Army-McCarthy hearings, Americans would see Joe as he was—an unattractive bully, scowling, impolite, intemperate—not as he came filtered through the files of the Associated Press, United Press, and International News Service. The menacing growl, "Point of order, point of order," became his ugly trademark. High-school kids began using the expression in mockery.

In her retrospective, Ruth Watt always described her boss, Joe McCarthy, as "a very kind man, very thoughtful of people working with him, but when he got in the hearings he was on a tirade sometimes. Whether he was playing to the press, or just taken with it, he did get off a tirade sometimes." Such was his televised tirade against the army for its tolerance of alleged Commies.

Cross-examination by Joseph Welch, the sixty-three-year-old, almost wistful defense attorney, was the legal equivalent of viewing a heavyweight counterpuncher KO an overconfident slugger. Welch brought out the worst in McCarthy, who rumbled into an accusation that Fred Fisher, a young attorney in Welch's blue-ribbon Boston law firm, had once been a member of the Lawyers Guild, an alleged Communist front. Fisher had indeed had a brief stay in the guild, long enough to learn of it and get out.

Explained Joe to Welch, his voice dropping with ominous sincerity, "I have been rather bored with your phony requests [to get] every Communist out of government before sundown." This was Joe's attempt at Senate sarcasm.

It was a needless, stupid swing by slugger Joe. The counterpuncher came back with an uppercut: "Until this moment, Senator, I think I never really gauged your cruelty or your recklessness. . . . little did I dream you could be so cruel and so reckless as to do injury to that lad." Fisher would remain with his law firm, said Welch, but "I fear he shall always bear a scar needlessly inflicted by you. If it were in my power to forgive you for your cruelty, I would do so. I like to think that I am a gentle man, but your forgiveness will have to come from someone other than me."

KO.

Scores inside the caucus room and the multitude of Americans in front of television sets watched this live drama and judged Joe McCarthy. Suddenly, he was the villain, no longer the hero, in a political morality play. Joe didn't seem to know what hit him. When Welch finished, the senator looked about the committee room as if seeking reassurance that he hadn't done something inappropriate. Little was forthcoming from either his live or his TV audience. McCarthy was in trouble, and suddenly he knew it.

Once finished in late spring and off the nation's airwaves—though still at the peak of public awareness—the Army-McCarthy hearings would leave Joe McCarthy critically wounded. Nevertheless, only the Senate, where no TV camera intruded, could apply the coup de grace. And the Senate remained unsettled in mid-1954.

To this point, the opposition's connection with Senator Flanders had been marginal. In keeping with the NCEC's non-partisan agenda, it had sent the senator a $1,000 contribution for his 1952 election campaign, which, scrupulous man, he promptly returned because he didn't need it. Not until mid-heat of the Army-McCarthy hearings did he figure in the NCEC Clearinghouse's strategy.

Lyndon Johnson had made explicit the need for a Senate Republican, not a Democrat, to lead the charge against McCarthy. Regardless of their common benefactors, Johnson had a visceral dislike of McCarthy, Rosenblatt said. But Johnson was a realist. Political survival took precedence over personal feelings. After his visit from Senator Hill a year earlier, Rosenblatt had called Johnson, suggesting that his leadership against McCarthy would show "the Brits and other sophisticates that he's not just another Texas cowboy but a major leader. He remained quiet, unmoved. We had to get a Republican."[9]

John Sherman Cooper, the Kentucky Republican, had worked with Rosenblatt in the effort to save European Jews—"a strong man." Rosenblatt turned to him: "'We need someone to cut down McCarthy's committee.' Cooper wanted something to work with. We drafted a motion to remove McCarthy as sub-committee chairman. Senator Cooper was with us, but the move didn't work." Help would come from elsewhere.

Ralph Flanders was made of different stuff than Lyndon Johnson. He might not have been a Senate power, but in Rosenblatt's estimate he was a tough man of integrity "acting solely on his principles." Aware of Flanders's feelings about McCarthy, Rosenblatt wrote him a flattering note, calling him a bipartisan hero who gave courage to his colleagues, and describing McCarthy as a "national problem along with the boll weevil, hoof and mouth disease, etc." The note was pro forma, perhaps an inducement, but not an invitation to join the opposition. It was the way a shrewd lobbyist lined up allies whose votes might be needed sometime.[10]

The two men would soon become allies, with Rosenblatt writing some of Flanders's material, yet Flanders marched to his own drummer. He did not await invitations. Early into the Army-McCarthy hearings, he made fun, of a New England sort, of McCarthy's investigations: "He dons warpaint and goes into a war dance, emitting warwhoops. Then he goes into battle and proudly returns with the pink scalp of an Army dentist. We may assume this represents the depth and seriousness of the Communist penetration in the country at this time."[11]

On June 1, 1954, Flanders, the Senate nonentity, made a speech suggesting a homosexual connection in the Cohn-Schine-McCarthy anti-Communist machine. Today, such an attack might seem crude and reflect more poorly on the accuser than on the accused, but at the time it was a bold volley, and one not unknown in McCarthy's own arsenal. "Does Cohn have some hold on Joe?" asked the senator. "The [Army-McCarthy] hearings are not going to the heart of the mystery which concerns personal relations." And Flanders kept going: "There is the relationship of staff assistant to the Senator. The relationship of the staff assistant to the Army private. It is natural he would want to retain the services of an able collaborator, but he seems to have an almost passionate anxiety to retain him. Why? And then there is the Senator himself. . . ."[12]

The innuendo in this speech inspired the playwright Lillian Hellman to label the dynamic trio "Bonnie, Bonnie, and Clyde." Others would call McCarthy's staff couple "the Leopold and Loeb of the 1950s."[13] This was long before the homosexual rights movement began to lift some of the stigma surrounding homosexuality.

In fact, not innuendo, the twenty-six-year-old Cohn was homosexual. He was a brat turned brilliant legal fixer in Washington and New York. According to Mark Russell, he had the boorish habit of eating food from others' plates in the Carroll Arms restaurant. Whether, as hinted, he and Schine complemented their work for McCarthy with a homosexual relationship is unknown. Cohn died of AIDs in 1986.[14]

The call to arms came on June 10, 1954. McCarthy, under questioning before TV lights and cameras in the Senate caucus room, was handed a note by Flanders. It said that on the following day he aimed to deliver an anti-McCarthy speech and move that he be stripped of his subcommittee chairmanship.[15] It is this way with gentlemen: give fair notice so that the assailed may respond.

The next day, Flanders "just came in and broke everything up," remembered Ruth Watt. "I thought Flanders was off his rocker. He interrupted proceedings. I was not impressed." McCarthy responded on the spot. He called Flanders senile and smirked, "They should get a man with a butterfly net and take him to a good quiet place." Flanders's motion would not carry, but the opposition had discovered their point man.

Ralph Flanders never flinched. On July 20, 1954, he served notice to the Senate of a second resolution regarding McCarthy's conduct, which was, as it said, "unbecoming a member of the U.S. Senate, contrary to senatorial traditions and tends to bring the Senate into disrepute. . . . such conduct is hereby condemned."

The nation snapped to attention. So did major players in the Republican establishment. Quickened by the resolution, Maurice Rosenblatt, too, came calling. Waiting in Senator Flanders's outer office, he watched the powerful treasury secretary, George Humphrey, walk in. In a short while, Humphrey, homburg in hand, stalked out, unsmiling, "looking neither left nor right."

"You could feel the heat," Rosenblatt recalled. "When I entered his private office Flanders was smiling. Humphrey had told him to defer the censure motion, to put it off in favor of an agriculture bill. I asked, 'What did you say?' Flanders said, 'No, I think the crops will grow anyhow.'"

Then came Senators Irving Ives, Leverett Saltonstall, and H. Alexander Smith, "the pallbearers," as Rosenblatt called the GOP moderates, none of them very friendly with Joe McCarthy but all of them fearful of him. Maurice quoted Flanders as saying that the three believed that despite their dislike for McCarthy, a censure vote would cost them reelection, so please, they urged, drop it. "What made you invent that thing [the censure motion]?" Smith asked Flanders. "You know I am an inventor— I've got twenty-two patents," he answered. Saltonstall's appeal almost brought him to tears. "I have no choice," Flanders finally answered. "This [censure motion] is a moral imperative."[16]

By this time Joe McCarthy had greater national renown than Dwight Eisenhower, Franklin Roosevelt, and Al Canwell combined. Ralph Flanders? Out in California, the *Sacramento Bee* commented that "when he launched his campaign to censure McCarthy, Flanders rose like a genie from a cracker barrel without warning or sufficient preparation for the role."[17]

Colonel McCormick's *Chicago Tribune* knew better. The day after Flanders served notice, the *Tribune* carried a banner headline across page one: "Bare Lobby Plot to Condemn McCarthy." Under it, reporter Willard Edwards revealed that "so-called liberals," working from suite 303 in the Carroll Arms Hotel, were behind Flanders's resolution of condemnation. Edwards accurately reported that the "well-heeled" group included Studebaker autos chairman Paul Hoffman; Arthur Schlesinger Jr., co-chairman of the "leftist" Americans for Democratic Action

(ADA); John Cowles and Ralph McGill, newspaper editor-publishers; union leaders Walter Reuther and Albert Hayes; and a dozen other members of the American establishment.

"This organization is functioning under the directorship of Maurice Rosenblatt of New York and Robert Sherwood, a playwright who once wrote speeches for Franklin Roosevelt," Edwards reported, half right. Sherwood was a name on the letterhead. He also noted that Senate majority leader William Knowland had gotten it wrong when he cited the AFL-CIO and the ADA as chief plotters behind the anti-McCarthy campaign. It was, Edwards corrected, "the National Committee for an Effective Congress."[18]

Edwards's tale wasn't exactly a major scoop. Although he played it in a low key, Rosenblatt never tried to hide the NCEC campaign. But having Flanders out front, carrying the campaign against McCarthy, certainly came as a surprise to conservative readers of the *Tribune*.

A stealth warrior, a Republican conservative, Flanders was anything but a liberal à la Herbert Lehman or William Benton. Edwards got it right about Flanders's support from the NCEC Clearinghouse—facts, speechwriters, lobbying forces on Capitol Hill, political backup for his campaign. "I was well-prepared by the NCEC," Flanders would say. "I gratefully accepted their help."[19]

Rosenblatt had advance notice of the Flanders resolution. On the day of its presentation, Maurice wrote to Dean Clara Mayer of the New School for Social Research in New York City that "the situation is ripe for a showdown with McCarthy. Television has unmasked his personality, which the press had concealed." A few days later he reminded "the Leader," Lyndon Johnson, that as requested, a Republican was leading the charge against Joe. Thus, he said, "it's time for the Democratic leadership to take a stand."[20]

Internal memos written by Rosenblatt at this time characterize Flanders as "completely motivated by principle," while congressional Democrats are "milling around without leadership or purpose." Lyndon Johnson had yet to act against McCarthy, and he would never get in front of this campaign as he would do as the American president in 1964 on behalf of civil rights. "The Senate has come to act like a Greek tragedy," said Senator Paul Douglas. "All the action takes place offstage, before the play begins."[21] This was a remark aimed at Johnson's backroom manipulations. But in the case of Joe McCarthy, it was better applied to the NCEC.

"Most significant," wrote Rosenblatt—witness to Vienna in the 1920s and New York in the 1930s—"is the inability of Americans to see the totalitarian menace" posed by McCarthy-ism. In the wake of Flanders's resolution, Rosenblatt said the task was "essentially a job of publicity and pressure—to work the [congressional] representatives, befriend the press, pressure Republican leaders—John McCloy, Paul Hoffman, C. D. Jackson [a Luce publisher]—publicize Flanders. The ball is in play. Can we score?"[22]

Senator McClellan had come around. He told Ruth Watt, "I'm fond of Joe McCarthy, but he's getting out of hand and we have to do something to control him."

The Senate punted. Instead of acting on the resolution, it assigned the matter to a select committee chaired by Arthur Watkins, a Utah Mormon, for "study." Wisely, Johnson named three conservative Democrats to serve under Senator Watkins, an "Old Testament kind of man, a hanging judge," in Rosenblatt's description, who "got under McCarthy's skin. Joe didn't hate Flanders. He hated Watkins."

While the selects deliberated, Rosenblatt warned Flanders to expect a counterattack from McCarthyites. No sooner warned than a California woman wrote to the Vermonter, "I hope God strikes you dead for your wicked attack on Senator McCarthy."[23] But a Senate counterattack never materialized. The floor of McCarthy's support inside and outside Congress had collapsed.

McCarthy made his usual show of forceful imprudence before the select committee. This time it backfired. With attorney Edward Bennett Williams at his side, he launched a tirade against Senator Edwin Johnson of Colorado, calling him a biased partisan unfit to serve on the committee. He demanded that Johnson be removed.

It was too much. "Out of order," gaveled chairman Watkins, who went on to rebuke McCarthy for his accusation against Johnson. "Shut up and sit down." McCarthy was stunned. For perhaps the last time, Joe McCarthy had overstepped. "This is the most unheard thing I ever heard of," he retorted.[24]

Joe was whipped. His stammering response to Watkins showed it. Passage of the censure resolution was now a formality. When his "condemnation" was approved by the Senate, sixty-seven to twenty-two, on December 2, Joe quipped, "It was not exactly a vote of confidence, but I don't feel like I was lynched."[25]

By that time he had come to understand the force behind that fatal Senate vote. Speaking of himself in the third person, à la Julius Caesar, McCarthy told Scripps-Howard columnist Arthur Edson, "The National Committee for an Effective Congress and Maurice Rosenblatt masterminded the censure of Joe McCarthy."[26] Rosenblatt said he had never received a greater compliment.

Joe's days as America's greatest demagogue were done. "It was very sad," Ruth Watt remembered. "After the censure the press completely ignored him. If he sent out a press release you never saw it unless it was on the back page—and he was into the press stuff pretty much, I think it had gotten into his blood. He didn't get invitations. I think it affected him greatly. I think it broke his heart, really."

Soon after the censure President Eisenhower, who didn't like McCarthy, sent invitations to a White House party to every member of the Senate save one. In anticipation, McCarthy had an aide sit by his office telephone awaiting his call. It never came. Ruth Watt remembered: "Senator McCarthy kept calling me and saying, 'Ruthie, go ask Mary Driscoll [a secretary] if I've heard from the White House yet, if I've gotten an invitation.' I'd call Mary and she would say, 'You know very well he hasn't—he's not going to get an invitation to that party tonight.'"

But if Joe was finished, his legacy to American politics was not. McCarthyism was too hot to cool down.

A pro-Joe counterattack targeted the NCEC, accompanied by the heavy metal music of anti-Semitism. "Why are [enemies of the United States] spending millions of dollars in propaganda and smear techniques against [Senator William] Jenner, Joe McCarthy and J. Edgar Hoover?" asked *The Cross and the Flag*, organ of Gerald L. K. Smith's "Christian National Crusade." "Treason is the answer. Flanders' speech was done under the pressure of a special committee headed by a Jew whose name is Rosenblatt. The mystery of the hour is the strange and secret way forces mobilized against McCarthy without the Communist Party or its fronts."[27]

"My Dear Morrie," opened a letter to Rosenblatt from one Julian von Alpenfels of Cicero, Illinois, no doubt a reader of the mighty *Tribune*. "I have followed with great interest the noble work you are doing in conjunction with the stupid Gentile stooges, like Flanders, Hoffman and others, to drive McCarthy from the scene.

"Has the senator from Wisconsin uncovered too many Communist kikes in government? . . . really surprising, isn't it, the number of sheenies pulled out of the woodwork, like the vermin they are, by committees engaged in ousting subversives." Von Alpenfels's signature was floridly beautiful. Rosenblatt had no recollection of having known the man.[28]

Hearst went to banner headlines at the turn of events. The New York *Journal-American* led its editions on December 4, 1954, the day of the vote on the censure resolution, with: "Link Leftist Group to McCarthy Censure." Backup for that headline was a story by Hearst's Washington bureau chief, David Sentner, saying that unnamed "McCarthy investigators" had found that "24 of the 39 NCEC board members are affiliated with pro-Communist groups" and that Senator Everett Dirksen of Illinois had labeled the NCEC "left-wing" and "in bed with Flanders to get McCarthy." What the NCEC really aimed to do, concluded Sentner, was "to stifle the investigation of Communism."[29]

Next day the *Journal-American* followed up its allegation with another banner: "Leftist Foes of McCarthy Face Congressional Probe." Again, no names, but a report that "McCarthy supporters" planned to push for a probe of the NCEC to determine whether it had violated anti-lobbying laws.[30] The newspaper stretched it with this piece. It had the credibility of Capitol corridor speculation hyped into headlines, perhaps by wishful thinking. But nothing happened.

Two years later, Joe's sidekick Senator Jenner of Indiana called for a probe of the NCEC. There was no response, save for a few back-page stories in the usual newspapers. This stirred Fulton Lewis Jr., a widely circulated right-wing columnist, to write: "The National Committee for an Effective Congress, a shadowy lobby for so-called liberal causes, used Flanders to paralyze the work of the Senate investigation of Communism and to destroy the chairman of the committee, Joe McCarthy . . . it [also] operates as [an] assassination cabal against anti-Communist candidates for Congress."[31]

Still no response to Jenner's call for a probe.

"Don't quit the fight," Rosenblatt cautioned the other major Chicago newspaper publisher, Marshall Field. "The Cromelin-Stratemeyer 'Committee for Ten Million Signatures for McCarthy' is under way, a nationalistic group pushing for preventive war [against China] in Asia."[32] A dynamic duo of the far right, retired Admiral John Cromelin and retired Air Force General George Stratemeyer were World War II heroes bonded in their fear of democracy as well as of Communism. Testifying before Senator McCarran's subcommittee on internal security in 1954, Stratemeyer allowed that "right up to this minute, there is some hidden force, some hidden power, or something, that is influencing our people. They don't act like Americans. Americans are supposed to have guts, and our policy is wishy-washy, appeasing."[33]

Despite the bluster, nothing happened to rally ten million to save Joe McCarthy or to heed the call of the China Lobby for war against Red China on behalf of Chiang Kai-shek, the fallen Chinese leader now in refuge on Formosa (Taiwan).

And Joe was fading faster than his friends.

On October 2, McCarthy turned up sick. He said his nerves were "shot," and he was hospitalized at the Bethesda Naval Hospital. Nerves or booze? McCarthy made no effort to hide his increasing taste for hard liquor. Evenings downstairs at the Carroll Arms were getting longer.

Down, but out of the hospital in mid-December 1954, McCarthy made a Senate floor speech calling for a blockade of Red China and demanding that the U.S. "unleash Chiang Kai-shek" from his Taiwan fortress to "attack the soft underbelly of China." He was carrying the cause of his friends Cromelin and Stratemeyer and the China Lobby. When Eisenhower, who had passed up the chance to rebuke McCarthy in 1952, refused to heed this call for war with China, McCarthy snarled at the president's "shrinking show of weakness towards combating Communism."[34] Was anybody still listening?

In June 1955, as Eisenhower prepared to meet Soviet leaders in a summit conference in Geneva, McCarthy offered a resolution to the Senate aimed at limiting the president's freedom to negotiate. For openers, it commanded that Eisenhower discuss the matter of East European satellites with the Soviets before the conference could commence. It looked as if it might be comeback time for Tailgunner Joe, a show of force on the Senate floor he had once dominated, a reminder and a renewal of the power of fear. The resolution failed, seventy-seven to four. Three of what Rosenblatt had called the Snaggle-Tooth Gang—Mollie Malone, William Jenner, and William Langer—stuck with their leader. The rest rejected him.

McCarthy was humiliated and, worse, isolated. He was also drinking harder, fading fast toward death from a whisky-diseased liver. "By the end of 1955 he was in pretty bad shape and we knew he had cirrhosis of the liver," said his friend Ruth Watt. "I was told that he told Senator McClellan that he knew he had something and was not going to get any better." He died two years later.

"He never believed his colleagues could—or would—do it [censure him]," wrote Fulton Lewis. "When it happened, he was a changed and a disillusioned man. . . . it was all done under a sinister, unseen, outside pressure . . . a shadowy, unidentifiable group called the National Committee for an Effective Congress, without fingerprints, pushing the feeble and aging Flanders."[35]

Flanders, the antagonist, had a kinder, gentler reaction to

McCarthy's death. He was "a man to be pitied," said Flanders. "He had a deep inferiority complex. For this he found relief in bullying witnesses, slamming associates, and garnering headlines."[36]

Decades later, when the public memory of McCarthy had dimmed to a twilight, Maurice Rosenblatt reflected on his role in the demise of the demagogue's assault on American civil rights: "The essential lesson learned at the University of Wisconsin, confirmed in the Bronx in the late 1930s, and finally applied to McCarthy in the 1950s is that the way to defeat an extremist is with the conservative establishment."

Easy to say, but getting church leaders and seminary students to oppose the Christian Front, and Wall Street tycoons and Midwestern industrialists to confront Joe McCarthy, took a political jujitsu artist. Such was Maurice Rosenblatt—in *Time* magazine's description, "an American original, a reformer in the great American tradition."[37]

What Maurice and the National Committee for an Effective Congress had done was to employ McCarthy's own excesses against him. They had a lot to use: ambition, scorn for fair play, lack of empathy, insecurity, and booze.

Epilogue

LONG AFTER THE FEDERAL COURTS corrected its excesses, the worst being a denial of due process in proceedings against an accused, the frost of McCarthyism continued to chill dissent in the United States. It took perhaps a generation to thaw.

Fear of heterodoxy lingered, as in, "My God, maybe I'd better cool my opinions—I could be named." The House Un-American Activities Committee, especially under a hustling former FBI agent, Representative Harold Velde, kept up the hunt for Commies—real or suspect—as well as for publicity. But the main event was over. The big tent of this political circus had gone down with Joe McCarthy.

"It took a long time for the country to recover," observed Maurice Rosenblatt, retired and reflective. "For a time nobody knew where they stood in the Cold War orthodoxy."[1]

Could it happen again? That question about American democracy also lingered. "Personally, I felt enormous relief," said Maurice. "I slept better. I recognized we were the instrument of McCarthy's destruction, but I felt no guilt. Just fatigue and relief. I was exhausted. I didn't feel like crusading again."

New York *Journal-American* headlines behind him, Rosenblatt took a brief fling to Las Vegas with his nonscheduled airline clients, payoff for his work obtaining certification for the nonskeds to fly passengers—$80 a ticket—between New York and Miami. There, in a temporary lapse of his normal self-discipline, he got drunk and married his companion, Laura Barone. It was Christmas 1954 and not a good decision. "I was always a rover," he said. A few months later, just as abruptly, they divorced. She died of leukemia later in 1955. Her memory haunts: "She was loyal and beautiful. I couldn't have done a thing without her." Rosenblatt would not wed again.

No more crusades, perhaps, but much more public business for a master of Capitol Hill's customs and corridors. Alarmed at the decline in numbers of American voters, he formed the Committee for the Study of the American Electorate. As usual, it had a blue-ribbon board, including diplomat Cyrus Vance, Abigail McCarthy, wife of Senator Eugene McCarthy, and Democratic political advisors Ted Van Dyk and Anne Wexler, and a cracker-jack director, Curtis Gans. Three decades later it remains in business (Maurice was president). Voter absenteeism still increases, but they are working on it.

If not a crusade in the mode of his past activities, Rosenblatt's lobbying on behalf of CBS, the television network, and its president, Frank Stanton, was a historic blow on behalf of the First Amendment, the right to free speech. In striking it—for a splendid $5,000-per-month retainer—Maurice saved Stanton from a congressional contempt citation and a possible jail sentence.

"The Selling of the Pentagon," a CBS documentary, followed the mode of Edward R. Murrow's "See It Now," his gloves-off exposé of Joe McCarthy, a damaging blow to the demagogue. Broadcast in 1971, the CBS show took the sheets off the Pentagon's huge expenditure of public funds to sell citizens on the Vietnam war—a sales job desperately needed, considering the war's unpopularity.

The Richard Nixon White House went ballistic. Hawkish Representatives Eddie Hebert, hotter than a Cajun sauce, and Harley Staggers, hard-nosed chairman of the House Commerce Committee, went for Stanton's throat. Hebert called it "the most horrible thing I've seen in years . . . the greatest disservice to the military I've ever seen on TV."[2]

Staggers got his committee to subpoena Stanton to come forth and bring all the network's notes and unbroadcast material ("outtakes," in TV jargon) dealing with the critical program. Refusing, Stanton faced a contempt citation and a jail cell.[3]

Stanton balked but did not fold. Instead, as Rosenblatt

recalled, the network dispatched "ten or fifteen lobbyists in Gucci shoes and a fleet of limousines" to work the House floor against the contempt citation, which had been approved by the Commerce Committee. The limos were conspicuous, lined up outside the Capitol's Cannon Building, where congressmen nested.

Someone wisely suggested adding Rosenblatt to the CBS Capitol lineup. Rosenblatt said he'd take the lobbying assignment, given a handsome payday—and provided he could order the others to keep a low profile, stop scattering money around the Hill, and take off those $200 shoes. In sum, move over and let a pro take charge. He did.

"They wanted to go for the liberals," said Rosenblatt. "No, no—you've got the liberals. You need Republicans, conservatives. The issue wasn't a matter of conservatives versus liberals. It was a matter of whether business, free enterprise, had a right to protection from Congress." Or so he framed the issue, and to work it he enlisted the support of several conservative businessmen. Political jujitsu all over again.

The key was Representative Gerald Ford, the House GOP leader and future president, whom Maurice, helped by those businessmen, turned into a supporter of the First Amendment, if not a fan of CBS. As Rosenblatt recalled it: "I talked with him in his office. He listened to me. He acted as though I was telling him things for the first time. Ford liked to look innocent. Sometimes maybe he was."

The Republican floor leader was one critical convert. The other was Wilbur Mills, chairman of the House Ways and Means Committee (the federal "check-writing" committee) and, no less important, of the House Committee on Committees, positions that made him a rival in congressional power to Lyndon Johnson.

Mills was educated and brilliant but fading from booze and his ill-fated romance with Fannie Foxx, a local nightclub stripteaser turned page-one celebrity for her fling with the former small-town boy from Arkansas. Mills, vulnerable, also succumbed to the charms of a high-powered communications lawyer, dispatched by Rosenblatt and concerned with freedom of the press.

The upshot: Staggers led the floor fight for his contempt resolution in July 1971 but came up short of support from Republicans—thank you, Gerry Ford and Wilbur Mills. He lost 226 to 181, a rare, if not unprecedented, repudiation of a committee resolution.

There are conflicting accounts of White House–CBS intrigue lying behind that slap at the powerful Eddie Hebert, chairman of the House Armed Services Committee, and Harley Staggers. No disputing it, a meeting took place between Nixon aide Charles (Chuck) Colson and Frank Stanton. Stanton's lawyer said the network needed White House help in avoiding congressional condemnation.[4]

Behind their meeting was Nixon's preoccupation, nay, obsession, with favorable treatment in the news. He wanted to pry sweeter stuff from CBS, and the contempt business pending before the House looked like a lever. Colson's version in a memo to his boss read: "If we help on the subpoena, Stanton will cut a deal—will play ball with us." Stanton's version: He promised Colson to give attention to any White House complaints about CBS but "made no commitments about news coverage." In his words, no deal was struck.[5]

Frank Stanton was rightly hailed as a hero for his fight for the First Amendment. Books and treatises followed in celebration, one by Garth Jowett duly noting the event's chief significance: "a clear statement that the networks could not be made to bend to government control in the technological era."[6] There's no mention in any of them of the CBS vice presidents in limos and Gucci shoes, Fannie Foxx, or even Maurice Rosenblatt, huddled over whiskey with Gerald Ford.

Having slain another dragon, Rosenblatt settled into lobbying on behalf of commercial clients, working from his handsome brownstone on New Jersey Avenue, two blocks from the Capitol and a few steps from the discreetly inconspicuous Democratic Club, where he frequently entertained. The Cold War dragged on in Vietnam, but relations with the nuclear-armed Soviet

Union eventually warmed.

By now, the usually reticent Rosenblatt had the eye of Capitol observers. *Time* magazine, in August 1965, had called him "an astute lobbyist with a green thumb for controversy." Writer Larry Leamer caught him better in a piece on Washington's power wielders. He quoted a parable from Rosenblatt's lobbyist playbook, a power story:

"There was a total power failure in this [mythical] town. The wisest and smartest engineers ascended on the power plant examining machinery, trying to get it working again. They could not. In desperation they called a university professor who asked for a hammer. With it he tapped a generator. Wheels turned and power surged forth. The lights went on again. So the professor presented the delighted utility bosses a bill: $1,000.07. Puzzled, they requested an accounting. 'Seven cents for tapping, $1,000 for knowing where to tap,' he answered."[7]

Rosenblatt aptly described himself in his own summing up, "Rattling the Cages: Memoir of a Passionate Citizen." He wrote: "I was a knight errant for democracy. I graduated from an academy run by Spinoza [the seventeenth-century Dutch pantheist-philosopher] and the Three Musketeers [fictional do-gooders]. My degree was in political realism."[8] Few in our democracy have put such education to better use.

Notes

MR   Maurice Rosenblatt

HUAC   House UnAmerican Activities Committee

LC   Library of Congress

NCEC   National Committee for an Effective Congress

NYCCC   New York City Coordinating Committee

NYC   New York City

NYT   *The New York Times*

Seattle P-I   *Seattle Post-Intelligencer*

The papers of Maurice Rosenblatt and of the National Committee for an Effective Congress (NCEC), placed together in the Manuscripts Division of the Library of Congress but uncatalogued, were examined by the author and by researcher Evelyn Braithwaite in October 2002 and March 2005. They are identified in the notes by box and folder number. The author's interviews with Rosenblatt took place at the latter's residence in Washington, D.C., in March 2001; February, May, September, and October 2002; January and May 2003; March 2004; and March 2005. They were recorded on seven tapes for approximately ten hours and are in the author's possession. Yet another collection of Rosenblatt's papers ("MR private papers") consist of uncatalogued letters and news clippings, which remain at Rosenblatt's Washington, D.C., residence. Uncatalogued papers of Harry Selden were viewed at his residence in Rockville, Maryland.

1 / The Carroll Arms and the National Committee for an Effective Congress

1. Interviews, Mark Russell and Maurice Rosenblatt, Washington, D.C., March 2003.
2. Interview, Woodruff Price, Washington, D.C., March 2003.
3. Interviews, Woodruff Price, Joe Miller, and Maurice Rosenblatt, Washington, D.C., March 2003; MR papers, box 54, folder 6. Rosenblatt himself quoted Barry Goldwater.
4. Interview, Joe Miller, Washington, D.C., March 2003.
5. Interviews, Russ Hemenway, New York City, July 2002; Maurice Rosenblatt, Harry Selden, and Joe Miller, Washington, D.C., July 2002.
6. Interview, Maurice Rosenblatt, June 2000. See also Harry M. Scoble, *Ideology and Electoral Action* (San Francisco: Chandler Publishing, 1967).
7. Interview, Maurice Rosenblatt, March 2001.
8. Selden papers.
9. Interview, William Henry, ex–Marine Raider Battallion (aka "Carlson's Raiders"), Seattle, July 1997.
10. NCEC papers, LC, box 5, folder 3; interview, Maurice Rosenblatt.
11. Selden papers: Rosenblatt to Seldon, November 1993.
12. Interview, Joe Miller, Washington, D.C., May 2002.
13. Interview, Theodore White, Cambridge, Massachusetts, March 1963.

2 / Tailgunner Joe, Chanker Jack, and "Moose Dung"

1. Jon Wayne Loftheim, "Hurley in China" (Master's thesis, University of Washington, 1973), p. 113.
2. See www.coursesa.matrix.msu306/documents/McCarthy.html
3. *Wheeling (West Virginia) Intelligencer,* 10 February 1950, p. 1.
4. MR papers, LC, box 18, folder 1.
5. Gore Vidal tribute to Henry Luce, PBS–Channel 9, Seattle, 3 May 2004.
6. W. Walton Butterworth, Oral History, 6 July 1972, Truman Library, Independence, Missouri.
7. Chiang obituary, *New York Times*, 25 October 2003, p. A29.
8. Interview, Maurice Rosenblatt.
9. David G. McCullough, *Truman* (New York: Simon and Schuster, 1992), p. 764.
10. Interview, Albert Ravenholt, Seattle, November 2002.
11. Interview, Ambassador Charles Cross, Seattle, November 2002.
12. McCullough, *Truman*, p. 475.
13. Interview, Albert Ravenholt, Seattle, November 2002.
14. Harvey Klehr and Ronald Radosh, *The Amerasia Spy Case: Prelude to McCarthyism* (Chapel Hill: University of North Carolina Press, 1996), pp. 8, 110, 114, 123-24, 129, 152, 217.
15. Klehr and Radosh, *The Amerasia Spy Case*, p. 124.
16. Joseph Keeley, *The China Lobby Man: The Story of Alfred Kohlberg* (New Rochelle, N.Y.: Arlington House, 1969), p. 3.

17. MR private papers: Pearson column in the *Washington Post,* 16 and 24 August 1951.
18. Keeley, *China Lobby Man,* p. 150.
19. MR papers, LC, box 14, folder 6: New York Times, April 1950.
20. Keeley, *China Lobby Man,* p. 3.
21. Ross Y. Koen, *The China Lobby in American Politics* (New York: Octagon Press, 1974), pp. 30, 178.
22. Barbara Tuchman, *Stilwell and the American Experience in China* (New York: Macmillan, 1970), pp. 525–26.
23. McCullough, *Truman,* p. 766.
24. MR papers, LC, box 12, folder 14: McCarthy floor speech, 22 September 1950; box 14, folder 13: McCarthy floor speech, 9 August 1951.
25. Interview with Albert Ravenholt, Seattle, November 2002
26. Ibid.
27. MR papers, LC, box 12, folder 14: McCarthy floor speech, 22 September 1950; box 14, folder 13: McCarthy floor speech, 9 August 1951; Thomas Reeves, *Life and Times of Joe McCarthy* (New York: Stein and Day), pp. 251, 255, 257.

3 / The "McCarthy" Elections, 1950 and 1952

1. Thomas Reeves, *Life and Times of Joe McCarthy* (New York: Stein and Day), pp. 129–334.
2. The Cousins quotations are from MR papers, LC, box 62, folder 3: Wisconsin State Journal.
3. David G. McCullough, *Truman* (New York: Simon and Schuster, 1992), p. 813.
4. MR papers, LC, box 14, folder 3: Wisconsin State Journal; Reeves, *Life and Times of Joe McCarthy,* pp. 334, 339.
5. MR papers, LC, box 14, folder 5: Raleigh (N.C.) *News and Observer.*
6. The McCarthy-Tydings conflict described in the following paragraphs is documented, as reported in the *Milwaukee Journal* and the *Congressional Record,* A7264, in MR papers, LC, box 14, folders 3–5. For the faked photo of Tydings and Browder, see McCullough, *Truman,* p. 814.
7. Reeves, *Life and Times of Joe McCarthy,* pp. 340–43.
8. MR papers, LC, box 14, folder 4: *Milwaukee Journal,* 10 January 1951.
9. Robert A. Caro, *Master of the Senate* (New York: Alfred Knopf, 2002), p. 142–45.
10. MR private papers: Rosenblatt to Brannan, June 27, 1950.
11. NCEC papers.
12. Shelby Scates, *Warren G. Magnuson* (Seattle: University of Washington Press, 1997), p. 151.
13. Ibid., p. 153.
14. Reeves, *Life and Times of Joe McCarthy,* pp. 450–53.
15. Selden papers, October 1952.
16. Interview, John Matchette, Palm City, Florida, July 2003.
17. Ibid.

18. Interview, Albert Ravenholt, Seattle, July 2003.
19. Interview, Joe Miller, Washington, D.C., September 2002.
20. Scates, *Warren G. Magnuson,* p. 137.
21. Interview, Maurice Rosenblatt, March 2003.
22. Arthur M. Schlesinger Jr., *A Thousand Days: John F. Kennedy in the White House* (Boston: Houghton Mifflin, 1965), pp. 12–13.
23. Caro, *Master of the Senate,* pp. 524–28.
24. Reeves, *Life and Times of Joe McCarthy,* pp. 468–69.
25. Stephen Ambrose, *Eisenhower* (New York: Simon and Schuster, 1984), vol. 2, p. 154.
26. MR papers, LC, box 19, folder 4: *Reporter* magazine, 21 July 1953, p. 9.
27. Ruth Young Watt, interviewed by Donald Ritchie, September 1979, www.senate.gov/artandhistory/history/oral_history/Ruth_Young_Watt.htm.
28. MR papers, LC, box 19, folder 4.
29. Ibid.; Reeves, *Life and Times of Joe McCarthy,* pp. 488–90.

4 / McCarthyism

1. MR papers, LC, box 54, folder 6: *Milwaukee Sentinel,* 7 August 1950, p. 2; *New York Times,* 29 October 1953.
2. MR papers, LC, box 14, folder 1: *New York Times Magazine,* 13 January 1991.
3. Ibid.
4. Eleanor Bontecou, *The Federal Loyalty-Security Program* (Ithaca, N.Y.: Cornell University Press, 1953), pp. 29, 31, 35.
5. The Silver Shirts had been organized by William Dudley Pelley, son of a Methodist preacher turned Hollywood script writer for Saturday cowboy idols Tom Mix and Hoot Gibson. See Karen Hoppes, "William D. Pelley and the Silver Shirt Legion" (Ph.D. dissertation, University of Washington, 1992), pp. 3, 46.
6. Bontecou, *The Federal Loyalty-Security Program,* pp. 352–57.
7. Interview, Del Castle, Seattle, March 2003.
8. David G. McCullough, *Truman* (New York: Simon and Schuster, 1992), p. 552.
9. Ibid.
10. Report of the California Senate Subcommittee on Un-American Activities, http://sunsite.berkeley.edu/uchistory/archives.
11. David Chute, *The Great Fear: The Anti-Communist Purge under Truman and Eisenhower* (New York: Simon and Schuster, 1978), pp. 394–99.
12. Interview, Irv Hoff, February 2003.
13. Shelby Scates, "Marine Oilers, Watertenders, and Wipers Union," U.S. Coast Guard Merchant Marine Document Z-948-754, Marine Firemen's Union B2540, 1951.
14. *Congressional Record* (Washington, D.C., 1950), p. 10794.
15. Scates, "Marine Oilers."
16. Interview, Maurice Rosenblatt; Edwin R. Bayley, *Joe McCarthy and the Press*

(Madison: University of Wisconsin Press, 1981), pp. 126–28.

17. Nicholas von Hoffman, *Citizen Cohn* (New York: Doubleday, 1988), pp. 129–30.

18. Senate Committee on Government Operations, Permanent Subcommittee on Investigations, 1953 Executive Session, vol. 1 (Washington, D.C.: Government Printing Office, 2003), p. xxv.

19. Bayley, *Joe McCarthy and the Press.*

20. MR papers, LC, box 54, folder 6.

21. W. A. Swanberg, *Citizen Hearst* (New York: Scribner's, 1961), pp. 477–79.

22. Ibid., p. 506.

23. Interview, William Theis, reporter for the International News Service, U.S. Senate, January 1969.

24. Von Hoffman, *Citizen Cohn*, p. 107.

25. Ibid., pp. 140–43.

26. Joseph Keeley, *The China Lobby Man: The Story of Alfred Kohlberg* (New Rochelle, N.Y.: Arlington House, 1969), p. 112; Reeves, *Life and Times,* pp. 248, 498–500.

5 / *The Hunter*

Apart from cited sources, the survey of American political extremes in the 1930s and 1940s presented in chapters 5 and 6 came from extensive use of the following books: David H. Bennett, *Demagogues in the Depression: American Radicals and the Union Party, 1932–1936* (New Brunswick, N.J.: Rutgers University Press, 1969); John Carlson, *Under Cover* (New York: Dutton, 1943); Ladislas Farago, *The Game of the Foxes: British and German Intelligence Operations and Personalities which Changed the Course of the Second World War* (London: Hodder and Stoughton, 1972); Richard Kirkendall, *The United States, 1929–1945: Years of Crisis and Change* (New York: McGraw-Hill, 1974); Rafael Medoff, *Militant Zionism in America: The Rise and Impact of the Jabotinsky Movement in the United States, 1926–1948* (Tuscaloosa: University of Alabama Press, 2002); James Ryan, *Earl Browder: The Failure of American Communism* (Tuscaloosa: University of Alabama Press, 1997); Howard M. Sachar, *A History of Israel,* 2 vols. (New York: Knopf, 1976–87); and Donald I. Warren, *Radio Priest: Charles Coughlin, the Father of Hate Radio* (New York: Free Press, 1996). Voice recordings of Father Charles Coughlin were provided by Richard Schrock, Seattle, 2002.

1. Interview, Maurice Rosenblatt.

2. MR private papers: *City Reporter,* 6 January 1942.

3. Niel M. Johnson, *George Sylvester Viereck, German-American Propagandist* (Urbana: University of Illinois Press, 1972), pp. 176, 181.

4. MR private papers.

6 / *Postwar and Palestine*

1. Ben Hecht, *A Child of the Century* (New York: Signet Books, 1954), pp. 484, 512.

2. MR papers, LC, box 79, folder 10: Bergson to Weizmann, 2 April 1945.
3. Palestine Statehood Papers, no. 690, Series I and II, Manuscripts, Sterling Library, Yale University, New Haven, Connecticut: Wise to Ickes, 22 December 1943.
4. MR papers, LC, box 79, folder 11: *Washington Post*, 13 October 1944.
5. Stephen Whitfield, "The Politics of Pageantry," in *American Jewish History*, vol. 84 (Simon and Schuster, 1986).
6. Ibid., 247.
7. Selden papers.
8. Whitfield, "Politics of Pageantry," pp. 221, 251.
9. Marlon Brando, *Songs My Mother Taught Me* (New York: Random House, 1994), pp. 107, 110.
10. Palestine Statehood Papers.
11. MR papers, LC, box 74, folder 4.
12. Richard Curtiss, "Washington Report on Middle East Affairs," May 1991, p. 17 (http://www.washingtonreport.org/backissues/0591/9105017. htm); David G. McCullough, *Truman* (New York: Simon and Schuster, 1992), p. 604.
13. Palestine Statehood Papers.
14. Curtiss, "Washington Report," p. 17.
15. Selden papers: Bergson to Rosenblatt, 27 August 1993.
16. MR papers, LC, box 74, folder 4.
17. Mimeograph pages obtained under the Freedom of Information Act; confidential telegram from U.S. Embassy (signed by Gallman), London, to U.S Secretary of State.
18. MR private papers; memo written by Sidney Wilkinson to Maurice Rosenblatt, March 8, 1947.

7 / The Cause

1. This chapter is based on interviews with Maurice Rosenblatt, March 2004.
2. Arnold Toynbee, *A Study of History*, abridgement of vols. 1–6 (New York: Oxford University Press, 1946), pp. 60–87.

8 / The Closed Hearings: Vengeance and the VOA

Virtually all the material in this chapter comes from transcripts of Executive Sessions of the Senate Permanent Subcommittee on Investigations of the Committee on Government Operations (4 vols.). The hearings, held in 1953, were not transcribed and made public until January 2003. Volume and page numbers of citations are given in the following notes.

1. Interview, Maurice Rosenblatt.
2. Vol. 1, p. 457.
3. Vol. 4, p. 3642.
4. Vol. 1, p. xix.
5. Vol. 1, p. 555.

6. Vol. 1, p. 573.
7. Vol. 1, p. 599.
8. Vol. 1, p. 615.
9. Vol. 1, p. 697.
10. Vol. 1, p. xxii.
11. Vol. 1, p. 673.
12. Vol. 1, p. 683.
13. Interview, Richard Schmidt, May 2003.
14. Vol. 1, p. 769.
15. Vol. 1, p. 787.
16. Vol. 2, p. 1440.
17. Vol. 1, pp. 13–31.
18. Vol. 2, pp. 1073–1114.
19. Vol. 2, p. 1231.
20. Martin Gilbert, *History of the Twentieth Century,* vol. 2, p. 857 (Toronto: Stoddart, 1999); Thomas Reeves, *Life and Times of Joe McCarthy* (New York: Stein and Day, p. 524.
21. Vol. 4, p. 3637.
22. Vol. 1, p. xiii.

9 / The Inspector and His Witnesses

Again, volume and page numbers in the following notes refer to transcripts of the Executive Sessions of the Senate Permanent Subcommittee on Investigations, 1953.

1. Vol. 3, p. 2667.
2. Vol. 4, pp. 3010–12; vol. 3, p. 2709.
3. Vol. 3, pp. 2701–14.
4. Vol. 3, p. 1919.
5. Vol. 3, p. 2175.
6. Vol. 4, p. 3285.
7. Ascoli papers, Special Collections, Boston University; interview, Albert Ravenholt, Seattle, 2003.
8. Vol. 4, p. 3244.
9. Vol. 4, p. 3013.
10. Vol. 4, p. 3023.
11. Vol. 4, p. 3296.
12. Vol. 4, p. 3566.
13. Vol. 4, p. 3573.
14. Vol. 3, p. 2551.

10 / The Clearinghouse

1. Robert Sherrill, quoted in Robert A. Caro, *Master of the Senate* (New York: Alfred Knopf, 2002), p. 542.
2. Caro, *Master of the Senate,* p. 547.
3. Ibid.
4. MR papers, LC, box 19, folder 7.

5. Thomas Reeves, *Life and Times of Joe McCarthy* (New York: Stein and Day), p. 296.

6. Ibid., p. 362.

7. NCEC papers, box 19, folder 7.

8. Robert Griffith, *Politics of Fear: Joseph R. McCarthy and the Senate* (Amherst: University of Massachusetts Press, 1987), p. 227; MR papers, LC, box 18, folder 14.

9. MR private papers: letter to George Backer; *New York Post*, 20 May 1953.

10. Interview, Maurice Rosenblatt; MR private papers: *Washington Post*, 9 June 1953.

11. The information about J. B. Matthews in the preceding paragraphs is from MR private papers: *Washington Star*, 9 July 1953.

12. Report of the House Un-American Activities Committee, August 1938, p. 915; MR papers, LC, box 54, folder 11.

13. This charge, originally made in *American Mercury* magazine ("Reds in Our Churches") was also reported in Reeves, *Life and Times of Joe McCarthy*, p. 499.

14. Manchester, *The Glory and the Dream* (Boston: Little, Brown, 1974), p. 700.

15. Interview, Maurice Rosenblatt, October 2002.

16. Ibid.

17. NCEC papers; Van Arkel to Benton, 26 February 1953.

18. Interview, Maurice Rosenblatt, October 2002.

19. Caro, *Master of the Senate*, p. 545.

20. Ibid., pp. 252–89.

21. MR papers, LC, box 54, folder 2: *The Cross and the Flag* (publication of Gerald L. K. Smith's "Christian National Crusade").

22. Interview, Maurice Rosenblatt, March 2003.

23. Rick Ewig, *Annals of Wyoming*, vol. 55, no. 1 (1983).

24. Interview, Maurice Rosenblatt.

25. Ewig, *Annals of Wyoming*.

26. Ann Coulter, *Treason: Liberal Treachery from the Cold War to the War on Terrorism* (Crown Forum Press, 2003), p. 104.

27. Ibid., p. 10; also Coulter, MSNBC, 7 July 2003, quoted "All Hail Ann Coulter," James Campion Hackwriters.com

28. *New York Times*, 20 July 2003, sec. 9, p. 1; MSNBC, 9 July 2003.

11 / Flanders and the Fall

Quotations from Ruth Young Watt come from an interview she gave to Donald Ritchie in September 1979, which can be found at www.senate. gov/artandhistory/history/oral_history/Ruth_Young_Watt.htm.

1. Robert Griffith, *Politics of Fear: Joseph R. McCarthy and the Senate* (Amherst: University of Massachusetts Press, 1987), p. 227.

2. NCEC papers, box 12, folder 7; interview, Maurice Rosenblatt, October 2002.

3. Manchester, *The Glory and the Dream*, p. 705.

4. MR papers, LC, box 54, folder 8: Washington City News Service.

5. Robert A. Caro, *Master of the Senate* (New York: Alfred Knopf, 2002), pp. 549, 551.
6. Interview, Albert Ravenholt, Seattle, March 2003.
7. Ibid.
8. NCEC papers, box 54, folder 8; Thomas Reeves, *Life and Times of Joe McCarthy* (New York: Stein and Day), pp. 562–63.
9. MR papers, LC, box 18, folder 14; interview, Maurice Rosenblatt, March 2005.
10. MR papers, LC, box 18, folder 14.
11. MR papers, LC, box 54, folder 8.
12. Von Hoffman, *Citizen Cohn*, pp. 230, 365–68; MR papers, LC, box 54, folder 12: Congressional Record.
13. Ann Coulter, *Treason: Liberal Treachery from the Cold War to the War on Terrorism* (Crown Forum Press, 2003), pp. 104, 110.
14. Von Hoffman, *Citizen Cohn*, pp. 20–26; interview, Mark Russell, March 2003.
15. *Facts on File*, 9 March 1954, 1 June 1954, 11 June 1954.
16. Interview, Maurice Rosenblatt, September 2002; Ralph E. Flanders, *Senator from Vermont* (Boston: Little, Brown, 1961), p. 267.
17. *Sacramento Bee*, undated clipping in MR private papers.
18. *Chicago Tribune*, 21 July 1954, p. 1.
19. Flanders, *Senator from Vermont*, p. 267.
20. MR papers, LC, box 18, folder 14: Rosenblatt to Mayer, 27 June 1954.
21. *New York Review of Books*, 21 November 2002, p. 14.
22. MR papers, LC, box 18, folder 14.
23. United Press (Washington, D.C.) wire service dispatch by Roy Calvin, 22 July 1954.
24. Reeves, *Life and Times of Joe McCarthy*, p. 649.
25. Ibid., p. 663.
26. MR private papers: undated news column.
27. *The Cross and the Flag*, MR papers, LC, box 54, folder 12.
28. MR private papers: Von Alpenfels to Rosenblatt, 13 December 1955.
29. MR papers, LC, box 9, folder 16.
30. Ibid.
31. Fulton Lewis Jr., Reading (PA) Eagle, 13–14 December 1955, MR papers, LC, box 23, folder 1.
32. MR private papers.
33. R. D. Mahoney, "The Tragedy of Southeast Asia," in *New American Magazine*, February 1, 1988, pp. 33–34 (*American Opinion* magazine reprinted by the John Birch Society, 19 December 2002. Appleton, WI: Publishing Inc.).
34. MR papers, LC, box 23, folder 1: undated, from *Washington Star*, p. 1.
35. MR papers, LC, box 23, folder 1: undated, from *Reading (Pennsylvania) Eagle*.
36. Flanders, *Senator From Vermont*, p. 268.
37. MR private papers: undated, from *Time* magazine.

Epilogue

1. Interview, Maurice Rosenblatt, January 2003.
2. Corydon Dunham, *Fighting for the First Amendment* (Westport, Conn.: Praeger, 1997), p. 16.
3. Ibid.
4. *Washington Post*, 1 December 1997, p. 1.
5. Dunham, *Fighting for the First Amendment*, p. 179.
6. Garth Jowett, "Selling of the Pentagon," in *American History/American TV: Interpreting the Video Past*, ed. John O'Connor (New York: Ungr Publishing, 1983).
7. Interview with Laurence Leamer, 19 July 2005, MR private papers.
8. MR private papers: unpublished memoir, 1984.

Index